# PARENTING THE GRADUATE

LIFE AFTER THE DIPLOMA

HOW TO MOVE FROM LIFE SUPPORT TO LIFE COACH

DRS. JOHNNIE AND TED SEAGO

# CONTENTS

# COPYRIGHT



Published in the United States of America by Greenlamp Publishing, an imprint of Greenlamp LLC, Orange County, California

Greenlamp Publishing
30021 Tomas, Suite 300
Rancho Santa Margarita, CA 92688

ISBN: 979-8-89962-068-3

# DEDICATION

*This book is dedicated to our children.*

*To our eight children—five daughters and three sons—you are the heartbeat of these pages. Through you, we learned the true meaning of parenthood: how to grow, how to pray, and how to eventually let go. Every season, from the earliest days to the proudest milestones, has permanently shaped our hearts and deepened our faith.*

*We also dedicate this work to every parent who has loved fiercely, worried deeply, and prayed without end. Whether you are celebrating a graduation or quietly navigating the uncertainty of what comes next, this book is written for you.*

*With love and gratitude,*
*Johnnie and Ted*

# FOREWORD

Parenting a child through graduation is one of life's great milestones. One season ends. Another begins.

This book was written for parents standing in that transition.

Welcome to the next season of parenting.

# INTRODUCTION

## THE CHANGING SEASON

Congratulations! You have successfully navigated the monumental task of keeping a human life alive from infancy to "baby adulthood." Whether you have been there since the first heartbeat or inherited a child somewhere along the path to the stage, well done.

No senior arrives at graduation as a "self-made" individual. Look at the name on that diploma, and you will see a mosaic of thousands of influences, prayers, and lessons. It didn't just take a village; it took a tribe of dedicated hearts to reach this milestone.

American author and poet B.J. Neblett once observed:

“We are the total of our experiences. Those experiences—positive or negative—make us who we are at any point in our lives. And, like a flowing river, those same experiences, and those yet to come, continue to influence and reshape the person we are and the person we become.”

This perfectly captures the fluid nature of identity. Growth isn’t a destination reached on graduation day; it is an ongoing, river-like process. This perspective eases the pressure to be "perfect" and replaces it with the beautiful reality of being "in progress."

For eighteen years, your graduate has been shaped by your influence. Now, as they enter this new season, they are still that flowing river—continually molded by the experiences ahead. Here's the secret: **you are entering a new season, too.** Parenting a graduate requires renewed intention, humility, and a willingness to grow alongside them. None of us is the same as we were yesterday, and this chapter ensures we will not be the same tomorrow.

### The Posture of a Learner

Parenting has always been a high-stakes calling, but parenting a graduate can feel uniquely complex. Expectations shift, authority changes, and emotions run high. Yet this season does not have to be a struggle—not if you embrace the posture of a learner.

Think back to the day you brought your first baby home. Most of us remember that terrifying thought: *Who would send a fragile human home with two twenty-year-olds?* That fear motivated us. We read the books, watched the videos, sought advice from "veteran" parents, and absorbed every bit of guidance we could find.

Parenting a graduate requires the same zeal. It demands a whole new skill set—one that many parents miss entirely because they assume the "training" phase is over.

### From Life Support to Life Coach

After nearly two decades of investment, it's tempting to believe the job is finished. The diploma is on the wall. The bedroom is ready for a fresh coat of paint. Case closed.

**Not so fast.**

Your responsibilities aren't ending—they are changing. For years, your role was **Life Support**. You provided the essentials: food, clothing, protection, and ultimate decision-making. You were the one keeping the system stable.

Now, as the mortarboard is tossed into the air, the "patient" is being discharged into the real world. Your primary role shifts from **Life Support** to **Life Coach**.

### Life Support

- Doing **for** them what they cannot do
- You are in the driver's seat
- You provide protection and oversight

**Life Coach**

- Standing **with** them as they learn to do
- You move to the passenger seat
- You provide perspective and partnership

You aren't exiting the vehicle, but you are handing over the keys. Like a trusted travel guide, you now help your graduate explore the landscape of independence—offering wisdom and asking the right questions without controlling the journey.

**What Are You Expecting?**

The "struggle bus" of the post-graduation months is usually fueled by unspoken expectations. To find harmony, we must address the "elephant in the living room":

- What does the graduate expect the "day-to-day" to look like?
- What financial or emotional support will continue?
- What does independence actually look like under your roof?
- What is changing—and, just as importantly, what is staying the same?

When roles are unclear, resentment follows. This season requires honest, "coach-to-player" conversations.

**The Road Ahead**

We've pulled out of the driveway six different times with six different graduates hauling a world of personalities in the backseat. Our high-top vans and packed-out Suburbans saw it all: we had the "High-on-Life" singer leading rowdy bursts of road-trip music, and the "Future Mother of Six" making sure every juice box was punched, and every seatbelt clicked. And we all know how hard those straws were to get in the juice boxes!

Between the dreamers, the quiet ones, and the rowdy ones, we had six hearts finding their own rhythm. We watched them all lean into the turns as we drove them toward the horizon of adulthood.

This next season will look different for every family, but it might just become your favorite season of parenting yet. There is a saying in leadership: **"Embrace the change that breaks the chains."** For years, certain ways of relating may have limited both you and your graduate. But like a fresh spring wind, a new season is arriving. New freedoms, new responsibilities, and new depths of relationship are forming.

**A Celebration of the Tribe**

Whether you are a parent, stepparent, grandparent, relative, or trusted family friend, God uses everyone in a graduate's life to nurture and shape them. Graduation is a celebration of the "tribe" that helped them get there, and that tribe remains vital as the landscape changes.

Through the years, we have watched many parents transition well. We have also witnessed painful train wrecks—relationships strained, communication broken, and expectations unmet. Our hope is that Parenting ***the Graduate*** will provide the insight, encouragement, and practical guidance you need as you plan the next steps with your "baby adult." We want to help you ensure this transition strengthens your tribe rather than straining it.

Embrace the change. Hold on tight. This new season may feel like a thrilling roller coaster—and it is one worth riding.

**Blessings and congratulations,**

*Johnnie and Ted Seago*

# CHAPTER 1

## FROM LIFE SUPPORT TO LIFEGUARD

Parenting follows a natural, sometimes exhausting rhythm. For the first decade, you're essentially a high-stakes concierge; for the second, you become a tactical lookout. Recognizing these shifts is the key to surviving the leap from the backyard pool to the deep blue sea.

### The Life Support Phase (Birth to Age 11)

During the first ten years, parenting is a long-term mission focused on keeping a small, chaotic human alive. This is the **Life Support** phase. Your role is straightforward: provide food, shelter, and basic physical care.

Throughout these years, you've been the ultimate safety net. You monitor vegetable intake (how many peas make a serving?), keep your child within arm's reach, and do your best to cushion every inevitable fall. You are more than a parent; you're the human bumper pad, the sharp-corner coverer, and the primary reason no forks made it into outlets. You're the source of all things—oxygen, Cheerios, and Band-Aids.

. . .

**The Lifeguard Phase (Ages 11–18)**

When the double-digit years arrive, your role shifts to something more elevated: welcome to the **Lifeguard** chair. You still provide the essentials, but now you're perched above the pool, metaphorically applying zinc to your nose and scanning the water for signs of trouble.

Your "Spidey senses" are now permanently set to "High." You're watching several bodies in the water, scanning for the rip currents teens often ignore until they're in trouble. In this phase, you'll be on the lookout for:

**The Digital Undertow:** The silent current. You're policing the "doomscroll," managing social media drama that feels like a Shakespearean tragedy, and trying to explain why certain TikTok challenges are essentially a Darwinian test.

**The Comparison Fog:** A digital mist created by highlights and filters. As a mentor, you help clear the air, teaching them that a calm surface on someone else's water doesn't mean there isn't a struggle beneath it.

**Mental Health Red Flags:** You spend a lot of time playing the daily game of "Is this just teenage moodiness, or are they drifting into deeper, darker waters?" It's the art of distinguishing between a bad day and a genuine SOS.

**The Social Whirlpool:** The dizzying cycle of "who is dating whom" and "why am I not in the group chat?" can pull a teen under faster than a physical wave. You're watching for signs of social exhaustion and withdrawal.

**The Academic Reefs:** These are the hidden rocks—standardized tests, college apps, and that one chemistry class that threatens to wreck the ship. You provide the lighthouse (tutors/schedules), but they have to keep paddling.

**Substance Interests:** Staying alert to vapes, "edibles," and modern entry points that look nothing like the "Just Say No" pamphlets from our youth.

**The Invisible Protection Dome:** This is your "stealth mode" parenting—vetting the houses they visit, steering them clear of toxic relationships, and being the judgment-free emergency exit they can call when a party goes sideways at 11:00 p.m.

## A Note to the Tribe

If your time on the lifeguard stand was relatively quiet—if your kid stayed near the steps and didn't try to do a backflip into the shallow end—congratulations! That is a massive blessing. Take a breath and enjoy the view.

From our experience, families with a "**True North**"—whether that's deep-rooted faith or a strong internal compass—have a steadier anchor. It provides a shared language for discipline, integrity, and right versus wrong. It's the lighthouse that makes the lifeguard's job less daunting when the fog rolls in.

We also want to give a special shout-out to the **Solo Lifeguards**. If you've been guarding the pool alone, we see the double-duty you've been pulling. It's exhausting enough with two people; doing it solo is like monitoring a crowded waterpark during a hurricane. You've been the constant in a life where others may have been absent. You've earned every bit of that "World's Best Parent" mug—and probably a long nap.

## From the Pool to the Open Sea

Let's be honest: Spending seven or eight years as a lifeguard is draining. You've spent nearly a decade in a state of constant vigilance, convinced that looking away for even a second could spell disaster. Your neck is stiff from scanning, and your whistle is worn out.

But graduation changes the scenery. The familiar pool—with its concrete edges and "No Running" signs—becomes the **Open Sea**.

In this season, your purpose changes. Remember: the Lifeguard's victory isn't in a child who stays on the shore, but in one who is strong enough to face the waves. You've kept them afloat; now it's time to watch them swim.

Your success isn't measured by how many times you jumped in to save them. Instead, it's measured by their ability to swim confidently and independently. The ocean is vast and unpredictable, but they are heading into it equipped with the skills you taught them from that high chair.

This new freedom—theirs and yours—is your hard-earned reward. Go ahead—take off the whistle. They've got this, and you've done your job well.

PARENT REFLECTION QUESTIONS:

1. **The Hand-Off:** Looking back at the **Life Support** phase, what is one "concierge" task (making their plate, waking them up, managing their schedule) that you are still doing, but they are now capable of doing for themselves?

2. **The View from the Stand:** Of the six "rip currents" mentioned (Digital, Comparison, Mental Health, Social, Academic, Substance), which one currently requires the most of your "Spidey senses"?

3. **The Invisible Dome:** Can you identify a recent time you acted as a "stealth mode" barrier between your teen and a harsh reality? Was that intervention necessary for their safety, or was it a missed opportunity for them to feel the "current"?

4. **The Emergency Exit:** Does your teen know—explicitly—that you are their judgment-free "emergency exit"? When was the last time you reinforced that they can call you from a "bad water" situation without facing an immediate lecture?

5. **Scanning for Red Flags:** How do you personally distinguish between "typical teenage moodiness" and a genuine SOS? What is your plan if you realize they are drifting into deeper waters?

6. **Clearing the Fog:** What specific conversations can you have this week to help your teen see through the **Comparison Fog** of social media?

7. **Checking the Anchor:** What is your family's "**True North**"? If a stranger watched your family for a week, could they identify the values that anchor your home?

8. **The Solo Guard (Reflection):** If you are parenting solo, what is one way you can "step down from the stand" for a moment this week to recharge, ensuring you don't burn out before they reach the shore?

9. **Measuring Success:** If your success is no longer measured by jumping in to save them, what is one "stroke" or "skill" (e.g., resilience, time management, moral courage) you have seen them demonstrate recently?

10. **The Whistle:** As graduation approaches, what is the hardest part for *you* about taking off the whistle? Is it fear for their safety, or a loss of the identity you've held for the last 18 years?

LOOKING AHEAD: **From Lifeguard to Life Coach**

The transition from graduation to what comes next isn't just a change in your child's schedule; it's a fundamental shift in your job description. In the upcoming chapter, we explore the move from the Lifeguard's high chair to the **Life Coach's sideline.**

We will unpack the "muscle memory" that makes it so hard to put down the whistle and the emotional grief of realizing you are no longer the "Expert" in charge of their daily survival. Most importantly, we'll look at how to trade **Authority** for **Influence** by:

- **Prioritizing Growth over Safety:** Learning why "controlled failure" in a safe harbor is better than catastrophic failure in the open ocean.
- **The Art of the Ask:** Shifting from giving answers to asking the kind of insightful questions that build your graduate's problem-solving muscles.
- **Retraining Your Reflexes:** Identifying the moments when your silence isn't neglect, but a vital investment in their independence.
- **The Sideline Strategy:** Moving from constant activity to intentional accessibility—being the mentor they *want* to come back to when the game gets tough.

The goal is no longer managing their days, but mentoring their destiny. It's time to move from the elevated chair to the sideline, trusting that the strokes you taught them in the pool will sustain them in the deep.

# CHAPTER 2

## FROM LIFEGUARD TO LIFE COACH

**From Lifeguard to Life Coach**

For nearly two decades, parents have devoted time, energy, and resources to life support and lifeguarding. During these years, parenting focuses on survival and growth as adulthood approaches. Parents make sure meals are served, curfews are kept, homework is finished, and hazards are avoided. Much of this labor is invisible, but all of it matters.

### The Seconds on Stage

On Graduation Day—at that single moment in time—a flood of memories fills the minds of moms and dads, grandparents, aunts and uncles, cousins, and friends. All have contributed something to this milestone.

- Teachers taught.
- Coaches trained.
- Friends influenced.
- Family supported.

Only a small circle of people engaged in the steady work of forming character, passing on values, and tending emotional growth. The walk across that decorated stage lasts moments, yet it symbolizes years of effort, sacrifice, and prayer.

Many in the audience recall both the good and the difficult days the graduate lived through, but only the parents witnessed the full story. They have seen the late nights, the struggles with friendships, the frustration over schoolwork, and the small victories that no one else noticed. Parenting is not only about preparing a child for graduation; it is about preparing a person for life.

### Building the Foundation

Personality and behavioral patterns tend to settle by early adulthood, allowing only gradual shifts afterward. That reality heightens the significance of parenting during late adolescence. While development never stops, the groundwork laid at home in these final years often becomes the lens through which a young adult makes choices.

A friend of ours is fond of saying, "Teens need your love most when they deserve it the least." Although maturing adolescents naturally seek independence and emotional distance from their parents, moms and dads should work to reduce that distance rather than widen it. This does not mean removing boundaries or abandoning wisdom; it means shifting how connection is maintained.

### The Grief of the Elevated Chair

The transition to coaching often begins with a quiet sense of loss. For years, your worth was measured by how much you were needed. You were the one who knew the favorite meal, the one who fixed the broken toy, and the one who navigated the school system.

Moving to the "sideline" feels like being fired from a job you loved. It is important to acknowledge this grief. You aren't just letting go of his childhood; you are letting go of a version of yourself. But remember: a coach isn't less important than a lifeguard; they are simply more sophisticated. You are moving from managing his days to mentoring his destiny.

### The Muscle Memory of Parenting

"The biggest obstacle in this transition is the deeply etched 'groove' of the Lifeguard habit. Your parental reflex is to jump into the water at the first sign of a splash. To move into mentorship, you must acknowledge that your instinct to shield them is now the very thing that might keep them from finding their own stroke.

When you see your graduate heading toward a "wrong turn" or a difficult consequence, that muscle memory screams at you to grab the whistle and jump into the water. Learning to be a coach means intentionally retraining those reflexes. It means realizing that your silence isn't "neglect"—it's an investment in their competence.

### Shifting the Message: From Reaction to Endurance

Moving from lifeguard to life coach requires a change in posture. A lifeguard watches constantly for danger and jumps in when trouble appears. A life coach walks alongside, helping the swimmer learn to navigate the water on his own. One role reacts to crisis, the other prepares for endurance.

Parents who stay stuck in lifeguard mode can unintentionally convey: "You can't handle life without me." Parents who move into life coaching send a different, life-giving message: "I believe you can learn to handle life, and I will walk with you while you do."

### The Burden of the Expert

As parents, we have "been there." We have the scars and the wisdom from our own twenty-something years. This makes us "experts" in life. The temptation is to hand our graduate a completed "cheat sheet" so he doesn't have to suffer the same mistakes we did.

But a Life Coach knows that wisdom cannot be downloaded; it

must be developed. If you give him the answer to every problem, he never develops the "problem-solving muscles" required for adulthood. You must trade the "Burden of the Expert" (telling them what to do) for the "Curiosity of the Coach" (asking what they think).

### The Tension: Safety vs. Growth

As a Lifeguard, your primary metric for success was Safety. If the child was safe, you did your job. As a Life Coach, your primary metric for success is Growth.

The friction arises because growth almost always requires a temporary sacrifice of safety. A graduate cannot learn to manage money without risking an overdraft. He cannot learn to navigate complex relationships without risking a broken heart. If you continue to prioritize absolute safety (Lifeguarding), you inadvertently stunt her growth. The Life Coach understands that "controlled failure" in a safe harbor is better than a catastrophic failure later in the open ocean.

### Trading Authority for Influence

In the Lifeguard phase, your authority was based on your position—you were the boss because you were the parent. In the Life Coach phase, your authority stems from your influence. Influence is earned through trust and the "True North" values you've modeled for nearly twenty years.

A Lifeguard uses a whistle to get attention; a Coach uses a relationship. This shift is often the most painful part of the transition because it feels like a loss of power. However, it is actually a gain in depth. When a graduate chooses to listen to your advice rather than being forced to follow your rules, you have reached the gold standard of adult parenting.

. . .

### The Power of Vulnerability

One of the most effective ways to reduce the distance between you and your graduate is through vulnerability. As a Lifeguard, you had to appear certain, strong, and in control to keep everyone safe. But as a Coach, there is great power in admitting when you've missed the mark.

If you jump back into the "pool" too quickly or misread a situation —perhaps overreacting to a choice she made or misinterpreting his silence—don't be afraid to own it. A simple conversation can reset the tone:

"I want to apologize for how I handled that. Just like I had to learn how to take care of you as a newborn, I am learning this new role of parenting a young adult. I'm a rookie at being a Life Coach, and sometimes I'm going to revert back to being a Lifeguard because I care about you. Bear with me while I learn how to sit on the sideline."

### The Coach's Toolkit: Asking vs. Telling

The most significant tool a Life Coach owns is the insightful question. You are no longer the one holding the GPS and calling out every turn; you are the one helping them learn to read the GPS for themselves so they can find their way when you aren't in the car.

**Try these coaching starters:**

- To encourage problem-solving: "What are two or three ways you could handle this situation?"
- To assess his own wisdom: "What is your gut telling you is the right move here?"
- To offer support without taking over: "How can I best support you in the decision you're about to make?"
- To evaluate consequences: "If you choose path A, what do you think the outcome will be in six months compared to path B?"

### THE SIDELINE CONVERSATION: **Accessibility over Activity**

In sports, a coach doesn't chase the player onto the field during the play; he waits on the sideline for the player to come back for guidance. To maintain a "Sideline Conversation," parents must focus on Accessibility over Activity.

This means:

- **The Power of the Pivot:** When he shares something, avoid the "I told you so." (Why make this about you being right?) If you pounce too hard, he will stop coming to the sideline.
- **Listening for the Subtext:** Sometimes "I'm fine" means "I'm overwhelmed, but I want to prove I can do this." A coach recognizes the difference between a player who needs a breather and one who needs a new play.
- **The "Game Tape" Review:** Help your graduate reflect on her experiences without shame. Instead of criticizing a mistake, ask: "Looking back, what would you have done differently in that situation?"

### THE SUCCESS METRIC: **His Character over Your Pride**

In the Lifeguard stage, a child's mistake often felt like a reflection of your failure as a guardian. If he got "wet," you missed the wave. As a Coach, you must shift your internal success metric. Your success is no longer tied to his perfect performance, but to his emerging character.

If she makes a poor choice and owns it, that is a coaching win. If she faced a consequence with integrity, that is a coaching win. When you stop worrying about how her life reflects on your "parenting stats," you are free to actually help her grow.

From the day they were born, a running commentary—sometimes praising, sometimes critical—has accompanied your role as a parent. As your child steps into adulthood, it's a healthy moment to release old regrets. There are no parent awards handed out with the diploma, only a new beginning to let go of harsh self-judgment. We all have plenty of "I wish I'd done that differently" stories, and often our grown children recall those same moments with more forgiveness than we afford ourselves.

### Delegating the Outcome

The final step in the Coach's transition is delegating the outcome. You have provided the training, the values, and the "True North." Now, you must trust the process. You are no longer responsible for his life; you are responsible for him as a mentor. This allows you to stop carrying the heavy weight of his choices and start enjoying the person he is becoming.

~

### Parent Reflection Questions:

1. **The Identity Shift:** Aside from being a parent, what parts of your identity have you neglected during the "Lifeguard" years that you can now rediscover?
2. **The Reflex:** What is one specific "muscle memory" reaction (lecturing, fixing, warning) that you find hardest to suppress?
3. **Safety vs. Growth:** Can you identify a current situation where you are prioritizing your teen's "safety" (avoiding discomfort) over his "growth" (learning from a mistake)?
4. **The Whistle:** When did I last intervene in something he could have handled alone?
5. **The GPS:** Am I letting her miss a few exits to learn how to reroute, or am I still calling out every turn as a Lifeguard?
6. **The Sideline:** Do I make it easy for my graduate to talk to me, or is my sideline "too loud" with advice?

7. **Vulnerability:** Have I apologized lately for "rookie" mistakes in this new season of parenting?
8. **Influence vs. Power:** Am I more concerned with being obeyed as an authority or being consulted as a mentor?
9. **The Game Tape:** Do I criticize the mistake or ask what was learned from it?
10. **Belief:** Have I told my graduate recently, "I believe you can learn to handle life, and I'm here to walk with you while you do"

LOOKING AHEAD: **The Pre-Talk Preparation**

As you transition from the lifeguard stand to the sideline, the most important "game" you will ever coach is about to begin. However, a great coach never steps onto the field without a game plan. In the next chapter, we move from the *philosophy* of the Life Coach to the *practicality* of the **Pre-Talk Preparation.**

We will guide you through the logistics of the "Parental Summit"—a purposeful meeting designed to retire the old parent-child dynamic and replace it with a strategic partnership. This chapter covers:

- **The Investment Audit:** A sobering look at the 6,500+ days and $300,000 you've already invested, and how to decide which financial support will continue and which will be phased out.
- **Managing the Mindset:** How to shift your internal mantra from "CEO" to "Consultant" so you can enter the room with a spirit of collaboration rather than control.
- **The Summit Agenda:** A step-by-step "Meeting Map" to ensure your conversation feels like a rite of passage rather than a trip to the principal's office.
- **The Coach's Toolkit:** Mastering the art of active listening,

paraphrasing, and open-ended questions to ensure your graduate feels heard, not lectured.

Before you can lead your graduate into the "Open Sea," you must first agree on the rules of the ship. This chapter is your guide to setting that stage with clarity, kindness, and respect.

# CHAPTER 3

## THE PRE-TALK PREPARATION

All coaches share one goal: to set players up to win. Parenting as a life coach follows the same logic. You have invested time, energy, and money to prepare your child for the next stage. Consider these statistics.

**By graduation day, an eighteen-year-old student has received roughly 6,570 days of care.**

For a child born in 2008, the estimated cost of raising them to age 18 in the United States was approximately $290,000 to $300,000, when adjusted for inflation.

### Expense Breakdown (Middle-Income Family)

The largest portion of this budget is spent on housing and food, which typically account for nearly half of total expenditure.

- Housing - 32%~$93,000
- Food - 16%~$46,000
- Childcare & Education - 16% ~$46,000
- Transportation - 14% ~$41,000
- Healthcare - 8% ~$23,000

- Clothing - 14% ~$41,000

We offer this data as a reminder of the significant time and money you've invested in your graduate's care. Even if they no longer sleep under your roof every night, some costs may continue—so it's time for practical, family-specific decisions about which expenses end and which continue temporarily.

Treat graduation as both a milestone and a reset: it's an opportunity to create a new framework for your financial and caregiving relationship. Start with two focused conversations that will occur in the context of a meeting.

- Caregivers only (parents or all adult caregivers): agree in private on what you will cover, for how long, and under what conditions (rent, utilities, phone, insurance, tuition, emergency funds, etc.). Set limits, timelines, and contingency plans.
- Caregivers and the graduate: present the agreed plan, explain expectations and responsibilities, and document the arrangement. Clarify what support is conditional (grades, job search, chores) and how it will phase out.

Putting these decisions in writing, with review dates and clear criteria for continuation or termination, reduces confusion and helps everyone transition with clarity and accountability. A template for this discussion is included in the Appendix section.

## Meetings

The word "meeting" can trigger mixed reactions. At work, meetings set goals and produce action plans; with your graduate, the purpose is similar—planning together, not holding a disciplinary hearing. Frame the conversation as an invitation to collaborate on next steps.

"The parent-child dynamic possesses a long memory. Even at

thirty-five, my successful son's first reaction to a meeting request was, 'Am I in trouble?' He still felt the phantom pull of being 'called into the office.' If an established adult feels that reflex, imagine the anxiety of a fresh graduate hearing the words, 'We need to talk.' To move from Lifeguard to Life Coach, you must lead with clear intent and a respectful tone: this isn't a reprimand; it's a strategy session for their success.

### Preparing Yourself

Before you schedule that huddle, you need to manage your own mindset. This transition is a marathon, not a sprint; your attitude sets the tone. Use these internal mantras to stay grounded and enter the conversation as the coach, not a manager:

- "My role is shifting from CEO to Consultant."
- "Listen first, speak second."
- "Progress, not perfection."
- "Clear is kind."

### Suggested Opening Lines

To avoid the "Am I in trouble?" question, it's crucial to relax your opening statement. It must immediately signal collaboration and mutual planning.

- "I/We need your help setting up a plan for the summer that works for both of us."
- "Can we grab coffee and map out what the next few months look like? I value your input."
- "Now that you're graduating, let's talk about the new rules of the road we need to set up together."

### The Summit: Setting the Stage for the Transition

Entering the Life Coach phase begins with protecting the conversation. Find a space away from the television and the household "noise" to ensure you are heard and understood.

Whether you choose the privacy of home or the celebration of a dinner out, the environment must be intentional. This sit-down meeting serves as a clear boundary marker: the old "rhythms of the residence" are shifting. You are no longer just managing a household; you are building an alliance with your graduate for the journey ahead.

### The Meeting Map

This is not a lecture; it is a summit. Much like international leaders exchanging tokens of goodwill to establish a "bridge of mutual respect," this meeting should follow a purposeful flow:

- **The Gift of Honor:** Begin with a gift. This time-honored tradition sets a cordial, positive tone. It is a physical bridge that says, *"I see who you have become, and I honor it."*

- **The Reflection of Pride:** Following the exchange, take a moment to express the immense pride you feel. While these reflections are a choice, they offer a space to ground the conversation in the graduate's unique history. Sharing "best life moments" reminds the graduate that your coaching is rooted in a deep knowledge of their character.
- **The Declaration of Shift:** The most pivotal step in this transition is the explicit acknowledgment that the old "Parent-Child" dynamic is being retired. This is your formal declaration that the "Life Support" of the last eighteen years has fundamentally shifted, making way for a Strategic Partnership.

This evolving bond is specifically designed to anticipate the challenges of the "Launch" and support the individual's movement toward the maturity required for a meaningful adult life. You are no longer just raising a child; you are commissioning a peer.

By using words like "The Summit" and "The Meeting Map," you elevate the event from a "talk about rules" to a "rite of passage." It feels more like a professional coaching session and less like a trip to the principal's office.

"Don't wing the first meeting. We recommend printing the '**Summit Agenda**' and sharing it with your graduate in advance. This simple step ensures that everyone arrives prepared and focused on the future.

### A Suggested Script

Mom and Dad might begin with something like the following script:

*"As a young adult, you are going to be more independent and responsible for your life choices. We have been your 'life support,' and that will continue for a season. But as parents, we are now assuming the role of 'life coach.' Our role is to help you navigate the next season of life, similar to how a coach leads his players to succeed."*

### The Coach's **Toolkit (Active Listening)**

Effective communication is a two-way street. As a coach, you must listen actively to understand his perspective, not just wait for your turn to talk.

- Paraphrase and Reflect: Repeat back what you heard in your own words to ensure understanding:"So, what I'm hearing is that you feel our current curfew is too restrictive for an adult."
- Empathize: Acknowledge his feelings without judgment: "It sounds like you feel frustrated when I assume you're doing something wrong."

- Ask Open-Ended Questions: Avoid yes/no answers; prompt deeper thought:"How might we balance your new job schedule with my need to know you are safe?"

### Living at Home Expectations

This meeting marks the launch of a new season defined by clear boundaries for both the graduate and the parents. It is essential for each party to understand which "life support" services—such as food, clothing, transportation, and financial assistance—will continue and which will be discontinued.

Beyond physical support, parents must determine which areas of the graduate's life, including career choices, academic challenges, and personal relationships, will now shift into a life-coaching framework. To ensure success in this next stage, parents must privately review all topics and reach a unified agreement on these benefits before presenting them to the graduate.

### Sample Conversation Checklist

Use this checklist as a starting point for topics to cover during your planning conversation.

- Communication Boundaries: (Frequency of check-ins, methods)
- Financial Expectations: (Who pays for what, budget roles)
- Living Arrangements: (Chores, guests, rent if applicable)
- Shared Responsibilities: (Family duties, meal prep, etc.)

Like most important meetings, this one deserves prayer,preparation, scheduling, and practice. As Brené Brown reminds us, 'Clear is kind and unclear is unkind,'* because clarity reduces confusion and prevents future conflict.

* Brené Brown, Dare to Lead: Brave Work. Tough Conversations. Whole Hearts.

**Parent Reflection Questions:**

1. **The Investment Audit:** Looking at the statistics of 6,570 days of care and nearly $300,000 invested, how does viewing parenting as a "long-term investment" change my perspective on the importance of a successful "launch" meeting?
2. **Addressing the "Phantom Pull":** Your son's reaction ("Am I in trouble?") highlights a long-standing dynamic. What "office" or "disciplinary" habits do I need to retire so my graduate feels like a partner rather than a subordinate?
3. **The Caregiver Reset:** In the private "caregivers-only" meeting, what is the one expense I am most hesitant to cut, and is that hesitation based on their actual need or my own desire to remain "needed"?
4. **The Identity of a Consultant:** If my role is shifting from **CEO to Consultant**, how can I practice "listening first and speaking second" during our next casual interaction this week?
5. **Environment of Honor:** The chapter emphasizes "protecting the conversation." Where is a "neutral ground" (a specific coffee shop, park, or restaurant) where we can meet that doesn't carry the "rhythms of the residence"?
6. **The Power of the Gift:** What "Gift of Honor" could I present at the start of our Summit that symbolizes their adulthood rather than their childhood?
7. **The "Life Support" Audit:** Which specific services (laundry, insurance, gas money, etc.) am I currently providing that are actually hindering my graduate's

movement toward "The Pulse Economy" of adult responsibility?

8. **The Clarity of the Script:** Using the suggested script ("We are now assuming the role of life coach"), how does it feel to explicitly say those words out loud? Does it bring a sense of relief or a sense of loss?
9. **Active Listening Self-Check:** When my graduate expresses a desire for more freedom (like the curfew example), is my first instinct to defend my "rules" or to paraphrase and empathize with their perspective?
10. **The Kindness of Clarity:** Reflecting on the Brené Brown quote, "Clear is kind," where have I been "unkind" by being vague about my expectations for their time or money.

---

**Looking Ahead: The Master Plan for a New Normal**

Having established the philosophy of the Life Coach and the logistics of the Summit, you are now ready for the most detailed stage of the journey: defining the "**rhythms of the residence.**" In the upcoming chapter, we dive into the specific **Discussion Topics for Parents** that turn abstract ideas into a functional, harmonious home.

This chapter provides the blueprints for "revoking the tourist visa" and inviting your graduate to become a contributing **Citizen** of the household. We will explore:

- **The Model of the Home:** Deciding whether you are running a "Bed-and-Breakfast" (service-oriented) or a "Working Ranch" (contribution-oriented).
- **Friction-Point Audits:** Practical guidance on the daily realities that often spark conflict, including laundry ownership, the "social glue" of family meals, and the "proof of life" text for safety.
- **The Bank of Trust:** How to manage house rules, curfews, and guests by trading consistency for autonomy.

- **Financial Guardrails:** Defining the "Citizen's Fee" (rent) and the line between Household Staples and Personal Luxuries.
- **The Working Ranch Agreement:** A comprehensive, written template to bridge the gap between "child" and "housemate," providing your graduate with a "practice lease" for the real world

By working through these topics privately before presenting them to your graduate, you ensure that you speak with a unified voice. This chapter is designed to replace passive resentment with clear expectations, ensuring the "Pulse" of your home remains steady through the transition.

# CHAPTER 4

## THE ESSENTIAL CONVERSATIONS

In **Chapter 3**, we covered the necessity of the "Parent-to-Parent Summit," but the importance bears repeating: **Before you meet with your graduate, you must first meet with each other.** Also, consider if other adult stakeholders living in the house should be involved in setting the new normal.

These private conversations are not about establishing control; they are about establishing clarity. When you agree on the boundaries behind closed doors, you can speak with a unified voice. This chapter outlines the most frequent sources of misunderstanding—the "friction points" that can drain energy from a household.

By talking through these areas ahead of time, you allow yourselves to respond with calm coaching and compassion rather than reacting with a frustrated impulse. Treat this as a starter list; adapt it to your family's unique rhythm to clarify what is negotiable and what is a firm requirement.

Ask yourselves: *Where did we struggle most this year, and which parts of our family "Pulse" need a reset?*

### THE CITIZEN VS. THE TOURIST: **Shifting the Household Mindset**

A helpful way to frame household expectations is through the analogy of the Tourist versus the Citizen.

A Tourist arrives with the expectation of being served. They treat the home like a destination or a temporary stopover, assuming someone else is responsible for maintenance, meals, and "amenities." Consequently, they often leave a trail of clutter in their wake, viewing shared spaces as someone else's department.

A Citizen, however, takes ownership. They recognize that the health of the community—the family—depends on their individual contribution. They don't just occupy space; they invest in it. A Citizen looks for ways to serve, noticing when the trash is full or the lawn needs attention, and acting without the need for a formal request."

### Auditing Your Home

Over the last four years, you have likely had both citizens and tourists living under your roof. If you are moving into a season with a "baby adult" back home, now is the time to be clear about which role they are expected to inhabit.

The transition from high school to graduation is the ideal moment to "revoke the tourist visa." By using this imagery, you can address expectations gently but directly:

- The Tourist Mindset: "I am here to be served."
- The Citizen Mindset: "I am here to contribute."

If you still have younger "tourists" in the house, introducing the Citizen image now creates a standard for the entire tribe. It transforms chores from "burdensome tasks" into "acts of citizenship." It reminds everyone that a healthy home isn't a hotel; it's a community where everyone carries a piece of the pulse.

### A Note for the Parent/Coach

Don't attack the character—address the posture. When the

kitchen is a mess, the Coach's question is simple: 'Tourist or Citizen?' This language gives the graduate the space to self-correct without feeling defensive.

Let's look at the specific 'Rules of the Road' for daily life where this mindset is put to the test.

### Engaging in Family Conversations

Every family has its own "vocal rhythm"—the spoken and unspoken expectations about everyday chatter. Take a moment to consider the natural decibel level of your home. Is it a place of constant casual updates, or is privacy the standard?

As a coach, you must decide whether you are comfortable with your graduate living a secluded, "siloed" life, or whether regular check-ins are vital to your family's heart rate. What feels like a minor detail now often becomes a major friction point as the graduate moves further into adulthood. When our youngest son returned home between semesters, we didn't impose a childhood curfew; instead, we asked for a nightly "proof of life" text by midnight. It wasn't about tracking his every move; it was about the courtesy of connection.

### Hanging Out with the Family

Does your family value "couch time"—those unplanned, spontaneous moments of shared laughter or conversation while the TV is on? While you can't force spontaneity, you *can* name it as a family value. By emphasizing that these interactions matter, you help preserve the "social glue" that keeps the tribe close during a season where the graduate's world is expanding rapidly.

### The Family Meal as a Cornerstone

Designating even one regular "Family Dinner Night" can be a powerful anchor. This isn't about mandatory attendance every single evening; it's about prioritizing a cornerstone time. Here is where the distinction is clearest: a **Citizen** gives advance notice if they can't make it, while a **Tourist** simply doesn't show up. Often, siblings crave this relaxed "hang time" above all else. Building this habit privately and consistently reinforces a sense of belonging that outlasts the transition.

### Bedroom Expectations and Cleanliness

There is no universal "right" answer here, only what works for your peace of mind. What level of clutter is acceptable behind a closed door? If this has historically been a battlefield, ask yourself: *Is the tension worth the emotional cost?* No one wins an award for the cleanest bedroom in a "failing" relationship.

If household cleanliness is a high value for you, consider a practical pivot: hire a professional cleaning service for deep cleans. Establish a simple system for trash removal and leave the rest to the pros.

**Private Note to Dads:** An affordable cleaning service is one of the most meaningful "Life Coach" investments you can make for your wife. To a woman balancing home, work, and a launching graduate, it feels like a birthday and Valentine's gift rolled into one.

### Home Laundry Services

If you've always handled the laundry, this season calls for a "changing of the guard." Use the summer to let the graduate take full ownership of the wash and dry cycles. Your role isn't to chase them with a basket; it's to coach them into a system.

The Coach's Script: *"My job is to make sure you succeed in the real world. In an apartment, no one washes your clothes for you. Let's set up a system now so you're never caught without a clean shirt for work."* This is also the time to discuss additional costs - who is buying the detergent, and who is mindful of the extra electricity?

. . .

### Contributing to the Upkeep of the House

A **Citizen** takes initiative. This looks like emptying the dishwasher without being asked, wiping down a shared bathroom, or mowing the lawn on a Saturday morning. These aren't just "chores"; they are the entry fees for living in a shared community. At the end of this chapter, the "**Working Ranch Agreement**" will help you formalize these contributions so they don't feel like random demands.

### House Curfews and Check-In Times

As maturity grows, the "territory" of freedom should expand. This is managed through the **Bank of Trust.** Every time a graduate does what they said they would—returning at the agreed time or keeping a promise—they make a deposit.

Small, consistent actions build a balance that allows for massive independence. Withdrawals (broken promises) lead to increased scrutiny. A nightly "check-in text" is often the perfect middle ground: it provides parents with peace of mind without making the graduate feel like they have a 10:00 PM bedtime.

### Friends Visiting or Spending the Night

Post-graduation, your home will likely see a steady stream of old friends and new colleagues. Decide the boundaries for drop-in visits and overnight stays *before* anyone asks.

- **The Citizen:** Respects the house rules and gives a heads-up.
- **The Tourist:** Assumes their friends are always welcome to the fridge and the guest bed without notice. Proactively set guidelines on frequency, notice required, and whether

guests are invited to family dinner to avoid awkward, unannounced "long-term" visitor.

### Financial Support for the Graduate

Money can create high drama when expectations are vague. Graduation marks an awkward season of financial "limbo." You must determine:

- Who pays for what?
- What income level is the graduate expected to contribute?

Financial support should function as a **partnership**, not a power struggle. Clear communication here keeps the "Pulse" of the relationship steady.

### Debit Cards, Cash Cards, and Credit Cards

Managing money is a critical milestone, and the tools they use are the primary means of teaching.

- **Debit Cards:** Encourage real-time ownership and balance monitoring.
- **Cash Cards:** Offer a controlled environment that prevents debt or overdrafts.
- **Credit Cards:** Most "Coaches" agree these should be reserved for **explicit permission** or pre-approved categories, such as school supplies, family errands, or emergency car repairs. Establish these boundaries early to ensure credit is viewed as a tool for stability, not a license for impulse.

### Establishing Communal Boundaries

Daily logistics—specifically the "snack situation"—can be a major source of friction. To keep the kitchen from becoming a war zone, define these boundaries:

- **Communal vs. Personal:** Designate which pantry items are for the "Tribe" and which are "Private Property."
- **Budgeting:** Who pays for the premium specialty snacks?
- **Restocking:** If a Citizen finishes the milk, they add it to the list (or the cart)

By explicitly defining these "house rules," you maintain organizational harmony and show the graduate that adult independence starts with how you treat the person sharing your refrigerator.

### Personal Care Expenses

As your graduate transitions into young adulthood, taking ownership of personal care is a practical stepping stone toward financial independence. While you may still provide the primary roof and "life-support" staples like toilet paper and hand soap, the graduate should begin funding their own specialized toiletries and grooming products. Distinguishing between **Household Staples** (provided by the Coach) and **Personal Luxuries** (funded by the Citizen) helps in three key ways:

- **Foster Accountability:** The graduate learns to budget for recurring personal needs.
- **Reduce Friction:** Parents are relieved of the fluctuating costs of specialized, often expensive, brands.
- **Establish Independence:** Making these independent purchases reinforces their identity as a contributing adult rather than a permanent dependent.

**Category Items to Purchase Independently**

**Oral Care** Toothbrush, specific toothpaste, floss, mouthwash.

**Hair Care** Specialized shampoo/conditioner, styling products, brushes.

**Body & Skin** Specific body wash, deodorant, face wash, moisturizer, sunscreen.

**Grooming** Razors, shaving cream, nail care tools, cotton swabs.

**Health** Hygiene products, personal first-aid (specific ointments/pain relievers).

**Optional** Personal laundry detergent (if they prefer a specific brand).

### Technology: Phones, Computers, and Devices

For Generation Z, technology is as essential as any other utility. However, the costs are high; research indicates parents spend approximately $1,300 annually on student devices. To avoid misunderstandings, the "Coach" and "Citizen" must define where the responsibility lies:

**The Goal:** Determine if a new laptop or a phone upgrade is "Life Support" (provided by the family), a shared investment, or an expense the graduate handles alone. Clarity here prevents digital drama later.

### Cars and Insurance

Transportation is a family-specific coordinate on the map. Is a vehicle necessary for their new job or degree? While some parents provide a car for safety and reliability, others require the graduate to manage their own transit. Before the keys are handed over, ask:

- Who pays for fuel and the inevitable insurance hike?
- Are there "Passenger Limits" (who else is allowed in the car)?
- Who pays the fines for a speeding ticket or a parking violation?
- What are the procedures if involved in an accident?

. . .

### MEDICAL, Dental, and Vision Insurance

Most graduates remain on family insurance plans until around age 26, but some may have school-based options. As a Coach, explore these options *with* them so they understand the value of the "Safety Net" you are providing.

### FAMILY TRIPS and Vacations

Travel becomes a complex puzzle once graduates start balancing work shifts and class schedules. Having raised six graduates ourselves and guided a few more along the way, we've learned that **creativity is the currency of connection.** Sometimes we flew a student home for a quick weekend; other times, we picked a central location everyone could drive to. We discovered a core truth: **we value time together.** Even imperfect, logistically messy trips build the lifelong bonds that will eventually include grandchildren.

### TRIPS Abroad

If your family values the educational impact of international travel, the "Tribe" has to do the heavy lifting of coordination. Planning these "Global Classrooms" requires looking months ahead at work and school calendars to ensure no one is left behind at the gate.

### BALANCING New Adult Lives with Family Traditions

When a graduate is away at school or working long hours, maintaining the "Pulse" of family tradition requires intentionality. To keep the bonds strong:

- **The Digital Check-in:** Schedule regular video calls to stay up to date on the "small things."

- **The Halfway Point:** Choose central locations for shorter trips to minimize travel strain.
- **Proactive Planning:** Put "Cornerstone Events" on both calendars months in advance.

### Education and Career Paths

Whether the path leads to college, trade school, a gap year, or entrepreneurship, the conversation should conclude thoughtfully. Ideally, the graduate leaves the "Life Support" phase with a direction, even if they later choose to reroute.

### The Coach's Script for Career & Stress

When your graduate faces uncertainty, your role is to coach the heart, not manage the problem.

- **Job Loss/Setback Script:**"*That's a tough blow, but it doesn't define your worth. What's our next play here? I'm in your corner.*"
- **Stress/Anxiety Script:**"*I can see you're carrying a heavy load. Let's talk it out. What's one small step we can take this week to lighten that weight?*"
- **The Reroute Script:**"*It sounds like this path isn't feeding your purpose anymore. That's okay. Let's look at the map together and see where you want to head next.*

### The Model of the Home

We have introduced the concept of Tourist vs. Citizen regarding participation in the upkeep of the home. Another way to look at your home model is to consider whether you are offering a bed-and-breakfast or running a working ranch. That simple question helps families decide whether home life will be primarily service-oriented (guests who are waited on) or contribution-oriented (members who work together).

- **Cleaning:** Define what "clean" looks like for shared spaces. Bed-and-breakfast standards mean staff (parents) handle deep cleaning; a working ranch expects everyone to wipe down counters, clean common areas, and participate in a rotation.
- **Laundry:** Is it a service or a skill to learn? In a B&B, parents wash and fold; on a ranch, each person manages their own clothes and follows a schedule to avoid piling up shared loads.
- **Lawn Care:** A tourist mindset treats the yard as property maintained for guests; a citizenship model includes scheduled chores like mowing and weeding as part of the "entry fee."
- **Kitchen Duties:** A ranch model shares the kitchen upkeep —meal planning, prep, dishwashing, and restocking staples

Framing expectations this way removes passive resentment. You aren't "making them work"; you are inviting them to be a **Citizen** or **Ranchhand** in a thriving community.

~

### Establishing a "Living At Home" Agreement

As stated earlier, "**Clear is kind, and unclear is unkind.**" When a young adult lives at home, a written agreement is a powerful tool to bridge the gap between "child" and "housemate." It clarifies evolving expectations and ensures everyone is tuned to the same frequency.

By utilizing a simple framework—"**If you provide these responsibilities, we will provide these benefits**"—you can effectively prevent confusion, reduce household friction, and foster a relationship built on mutual respect.

### TEMPLATE: THE "LIVING IN THIS HOME" Agreement

This document serves as a "**Practice Lease,**" helping graduates understand the mechanics of contracts before they sign an official apartment lease in the real world.

**Parties Involved:** [Parent Names] and [Graduate Name]

**Effective Dates:** [Start Date] to [End Date/Review Date]

### I. RESPONSIBILITIES (THE "IF")

- **Professional/Educational Pursuit:** Maintain full-time employment or active enrollment in a higher education program.
- **Financial Contribution:** Provide a monthly "**Citizen's Fee**" of $________ due on the 1st of each month to cover shared household expenses.
- **Household Maintenance:** Assume responsibility for specific chores, listed below, to be completed weekly.
- **Proactive Communication:** Provide notification of absence from shared meals or overnight stays by 5:00 PM.
- **Family Engagement:** Attend scheduled extended family events and holiday gatherings as a representative of the household.

**Religious Participation:** Attend weekly church services with the family.

### II. BENEFITS (THE "THEN")

- **Private Residency:** Exclusive use of a designated bedroom and shared use of common living areas.
- **Utilities & Services:** Access to internet, water, electricity, and laundry facilities.
- **Provisions:** Access to shared household groceries and family-prepared meals.
- **Autonomy:** Recognition of adult status and privacy, contingent upon the fulfillment of agreed-upon responsibilities.

### III. Vehicle Use & Maintenance

- **Fueling Protocol:** The vehicle must be returned with at least a **1/4 tank** of fuel.
- **General Upkeep:** The operator is responsible for keeping the interior free of trash and reporting mechanical issues immediately.
- **Insurance & Safety:** Any citations or insurance premium increases resulting from the operator's actions are the operator's financial responsibility.

### IV. House Rules

- **Guest Policy:** Guests are permitted until _______ PM. Overnight guests require 24-hour notice and mutual consent.
- **Quiet Hours:** Noise levels must be kept to a minimum between _______ PM and _______ AM.
- **Substance Policy:** No illegal substances or unauthorized smoking/vaping are permitted on the premises.

### V. Review Period

This agreement will be formally reviewed every **90 days** to ensure the terms remain equitable for all parties.

**Signatures:**

Parent/Coach: ______________________

Graduate/Citizen: ____________________

~

## LIVING AWAY from Home

Moving away is a major milestone. Setting clear financial expectations early provides a roadmap for success and protects the relationship during a time of significant change.

1. **Defining Shared Responsibilities: Sit** down together to decide which expenses are "**Life Support**" (rent or insurance) and which the graduate is ready to take on as a "**Coach's Challenge**" (groceries, gas, or personal items). Putting these limits in writing helps everyone stay on the same page.

2. **Navigating Shared Housing Living:** Living with roommates introduces "what-ifs." Discuss scenarios like a roommate moving out suddenly or a late utility bill. Having a "**Safety Net**" plan for these hiccups ensures the graduate knows they have a path forward when things don't go perfectly.

3. **Growing Toward Financial Independence: Schedule** regular, low-stress "**Budget Summits**" to talk about the numbers. This is a great chance to celebrate successes and troubleshoot challenges. The long-term vision is a gradual "hand-off" of full responsibility.

## INCOME, Tools, and Success

**Part-Time Work:** Many college counselors suggest working no more than **10–15 hours per week** during the first year.

- Encourage on-campus jobs to improve time efficiency.
- Set "**Blackout Times**" for study and exams.
- If work interferes with academics, the "Coach" and "Citizen" should adjust the shift load immediately.

**The 50/30/20 Rule for Budgeting:**

- **50% on Needs:** Rent, insurance, food, utilities.
- **30% on Wants:** Entertainment, dining out, hobbies.
- **20% on Savings:** Emergency fund and long-term goals.

STUDENT SUCCESS CHECKLIST **(The 90-Day Challenge):**

[ ] **Select Your Tool:** Use a tracking platform like YNAB or a custom spreadsheet.

[ ] **The "Every Dollar" Rule:** Track every transaction for 90 days. No expense is too small.

[ ] **Establish Your Baseline:** See where the money *actually* goes versus where you think it goes.

[ ] **Consult an "Expert":** If family dynamics make financial advice difficult, seek a neutral third-party professional.

~

THE "WORKING RANCH AGREEMENT" **Template**

This template helps clarify the "citizen" versus "tourist" dynamic. Parents can fill in the blanks privately and present them during their planning conversation with their graduate.

- Cleaning (Bedroom, shared bath, own dishes)
- Housing (Bed, roof, utilities)
- Laundry (Washing own clothes)
- Food (Home-cooked meals, basic snacks)
- Lawn Care (Mowing 1x per week)
- Insurance (Medical/Auto premiums)
- Job/School (Maintaining full-time work/study)
- Car Access (Use of family vehicle)

Add to this list...

~

**Parent Reflection Questions:**

1. **The Mindset Audit:** Be honest: Have you been treating your graduate more like a **Tourist** (someone to be served) or a **Citizen** (someone who contributes)? What is one specific behavior you can change this week to signal that the "tourist visa" has expired?
2. **The Model of the Home:** If your home were a business, is it currently operating as a **Bed-and-Breakfast** or a **Working Ranch**? Which model do you *want* it to be, and what is the first step to shifting that culture?
3. **Unified Front:** Where do you and your spouse/partner currently disagree on household expectations (e.g., curfews, cleanliness, or financial support)? How can you reach a "unified voice" before presenting these to your graduate?
4. **The "Pulse" Check:** Looking back at the last six months, what was the primary source of friction in the house? Is this a "negotiable" area where you can relax, or a "non-negotiable" that needs a clear written boundary?
5. **The Courtesy of Connection:** How do you feel about the "proof of life" text idea? Does it provide you with the peace of mind you need, or do you feel a pull to revert to a more restrictive childhood curfew?
6. **The Changing of the Guard:** Which "Life Support" tasks —like laundry, car maintenance, or grocery shopping— are you still handling that your graduate is ready to take on as a "Coach's Challenge"?
7. **Financial Limbo:** Have you clearly defined the difference between **Household Staples** (what you provide) and **Personal Luxuries** (what they fund)? Where is the line for items like specialty snacks, high-end toiletries, or streaming services?
8. **The Bank of Trust:** Think of a recent "deposit" your graduate made in the Bank of Trust. How can you reward

that consistency with an increase in their "territory" of freedom?

9. **The Working Ranch Agreement:** Looking at the template provided, which of the **Responsibilities** (the "If") do you feel is most critical for your graduate's growth right now? Which of the **Benefits** (the "Then") are you most willing to leverage?
10. **The Success Metric:** If your goal is to "commission a peer" rather than "raise a child," how does that shift the way you will handle the next mess in the kitchen or the next late-night out?

~

**LOOKING AHEAD: Navigating the Emotional Roller Coaster**

While Chapters 3 and 4 focused on the "hard skills" of schedules, contracts, and kitchen cleanup, Chapter 5 turns toward the "soft skills" that keep the family heart beating. In this final stretch, you move from being a household manager to an emotional stabilizer. We explore how to handle the "displacement behaviors"—those sudden, confusing outbursts that usually have more to do with fear of the future than a messy bedroom.

In the upcoming chapter, we will cover:

- **The Paradox of Firsts and Lasts:** Understanding the mental fatigue that comes when you are simultaneously mourning a childhood and celebrating a future.
- **The Science of Stress:** A look at the developing brain (the prefrontal cortex) and why your graduate needs you to be a "**Non-Anxious Presence**" rather than a problem-solver.
- **The Adrenaline Crash:** Preparing for the post-graduation "slump" and why a low-stakes, unplugged getaway is the best medicine for a frayed family.
- **The Coach's Communication Toolkit:** Practical, "ready-to-use" scripts for de-escalating outbursts, empathizing

with grief, and offering guidance without sounding like a lecturer.

- **The Discovery Phase:** Using summer work not just as a paycheck, but as a low-stakes environment for your graduate to learn who they are becoming.

This chapter is your guide to trading the "Lifeguard" whistle for the "Life Coach" clipboard, ensuring that when the "Open Sea" finally arrives, your relationship is built on a foundation of mutual respect and emotional resilience.

# CHAPTER 5

## NAVIGATING THE EMOTIONAL ROLLER COASTER

In **Chapter 4**, we mapped out the essential architecture of household logistics to foster a supportive environment. However, as the graduation stage is assembled and the reality of the finish line nears, the atmosphere in your home will begin to shift. Conversations that were once centered on the "vitals"—chores, grades, and schedules—may suddenly be swept up in a whirlwind of senior-year emotion.

**Chapter 5** dives into the emotional overload of this transition. Understanding these dynamics is what separates a "Manager" from a "Mentor." By learning to read the emotional gauges of your home, you can help your graduate transition into adulthood with resilience rather than just a diploma.

### The Duality **of Firsts and Lasts**

Senior year is a paradox of timing—a constant collision of exciting "firsts" and bittersweet "lasts." While students are submitting their first college and job applications, parents are meeting a new, complicated "best friend": the FAFSA.

These milestones are balanced by a heavy schedule of "finales"—

the last football game under the lights, the final homecoming, the spring concert, and the closing night of the theater production. This "living in two worlds" creates a unique mental fatigue. You are simultaneously celebrating the future and mourning the past, which can leave both parent and graduate feeling emotionally frayed.

### The Psychology of Sudden Shifts

As a Life Coach, your skills will be tested by sudden, confusing emotional shifts. You may find yourself wondering: *Where did that outburst come from? Why are they suddenly so clingy—or so distant?*

Most of these outbursts are rarely about the laundry or the curfew; they are "**displacement behaviors.**" The graduate is often terrified of the unknown future and takes it out on the one person in their world they feel safest with: **you.**

### The Coach's Insight

Anger is often just "fear wearing a mask."

Recognizing this allows you to respond calmly rather than escalate the conflict. This is the moment you officially trade your "Lifeguard" whistle for a "Life Coach" clipboard. Pride and panic often coexist in the same hallway; one minute you're celebrating an acceptance letter, and the next, you're navigating an argument over a messy room.

### The Developing Brain and Stress

It is a mistake to expect emotional maturity to arrive automatically with a diploma. In reality, the **prefrontal cortex**—the part of the brain responsible for impulse control and "big picture" thinking —is a work in progress until the mid-twenties.

Emotional overload isn't a sign that something is wrong; it's a sign that something **important** is changing. In this season, your graduate doesn't need you to be a "Problem Solver" who fixes their stress. They need you to be a "**Non-Anxious Presence**"—a stabilizer who remains steady even when their world feels fragile.

### The Life-Coaching Conversation

When emotions run high, your greatest tools are curiosity and silence. Instead of offering immediate advice, adopt a "Consultant" mindset. Pose questions that encourage self-reflection:

- *"On a scale of 1 to 10, how much of this stress is about the task, and how much is about the change?"*
- *"What feels the heaviest right now?"*
- *"How can I support you without taking over the steering wheel?"*

These questions keep the responsibility with the graduate while fostering a deep, adult-level connection.

### Creating Space to Decompress: The Adrenaline Crash

Do not expect life to immediately reset the day after graduation. The "adrenaline crash" is real. Everyone needs time to recalibrate.

This is the ideal season for a getaway—whether it's a beach trip, a mountain retreat, or a simple weekend camping. It doesn't need to be expensive; it just needs to be **unplugged.** Even a long walk or an unhurried meal can help your family stabilize before stepping into new responsibilities.

### Emerging Relationships and Social Shifts

As the graduate's world expands, their "Tribe" will shift. New social circles from jobs or college will gradually replace high school friendships. This is often a season of "**Anticipatory Grief**"—the mourning of a life that hasn't quite ended yet.

Some friendships will fade simply because paths diverge. You can help by:

- **Valuing the New:** Learn the names of the new friends entering their lives. Names carry weight.
- **Using Hospitality:** Invite new friends over for a meal.
- **Presence teaches more than probing.** Observing their new circle naturally allows you to see their character without an interrogation.

### SUMMER WORK AND DISCOVERY: **The Bridge to the New Normal**

For many, summer work serves as the critical bridge between the fading identity of a "high school senior" and the burgeoning reality of a "graduate." This season marks the first practical step toward a new normal—the beginning of life as a responsible adult, contributing to both society and the home.

### THE COACHING MISSION

If your graduate has already secured a summer job, your mission is to remain steady in your role as a **Life Coach**, offering encouragement as they navigate the professional world. However, if they currently lack a plan, you may find your patience being tested. In those moments of friction, it is vital to remember:

*"Not knowing" is not the same as failing.*

### THE DISCOVERY PHASE

For many graduates, a summer job provides a low-stakes environment to build confidence and, perhaps more importantly, to discover what they *don't* want to do for the rest of their lives. These early work experiences are as much about elimination as they are about aspiration.

. . .

THE COACH'S INSIGHT: **Forward-Looking Guidance**

Keep your conversations focused on the horizon, not the rearview mirror. Avoid dwelling on past stalls or missed opportunities. Your objective in this season is not to achieve emotional perfection, but to foster **emotional resilience**—a quality required of both the graduate and the parent as you navigate this transition together.

~

THE LIFE COACH'S **Communication Toolkit**

***1. When They Are Venting (The "Non-Anxious Presence")***

When your graduate is overwhelmed, the goal is to provide a "landing pad" for their emotions without taking on their anxiety.

- "That sounds like a lot to carry at once. I'm just going to listen."
- "I can see you're feeling the weight of [specific event]. It makes sense why that would be stressful."
- "Do you need to vent, do you need advice, or do you just need a distraction?" (This is the ultimate coaching question).
- "I hear you. I'm in your corner."

***2. When an Outburst Happens (The "De-Escalator")***

If a graduate snaps over something small (like dinner or laundry), it's usually a form of "displacement" for a larger fear.

- "It feels like there's a lot more going on than just [the laundry]. When you're ready, I'd love to hear what's really on your mind."
- "I'm going to step away so we don't say things we regret. Let's circle back in twenty minutes."

- "I'm not the enemy, even though it might feel like it right now. I'm on your team."

*3. When They Are Facing the "Unknown" (The "Stabilizer")*

When the panic of "What's next?" hits, use these phrases to ground them in the present.

- "You don't have to have the next four years figured out today. You just need to know the next right step."
- "It's okay to be unsure. Not knowing isn't the same as failing."
- "We've navigated big changes before, and we will navigate this one too."

*4. When You Need to Offer Guidance (The "Consultant")*

Shift from "telling" to "asking" to keep the responsibility on their shoulders.

- "I have some thoughts on that—would you like to hear them, or are you still working through it yourself?"
- "What's your 'Plan B' if that doesn't work out? I'm happy to help you brainstorm it."
- "What do you think is the biggest hurdle standing in your way right now?"

*5. When They Are Grieving "Lasts" (The "Empath")*

For the bittersweet moments of the final game or final concert.

- "It's okay to be sad that this is ending, even if you're excited for what's next."
- "You've put so much of yourself into this. It's natural to feel the loss of this season."
- "What is your favorite memory from this specific experience?"

**The "Golden Rule" for the Life Coach:**

Wait for the "invite." Advice given without being asked for often sounds like a lecture. By asking, *"Do you want my perspective on that?"* you respect their growing independence and make them more likely to actually listen to what you have to say.

PARENT REFLECTION QUESTIONS:

1. **The Mask of Anger:** Think about a recent conflict or outburst from your graduate. If you look past the tone of voice or the specific topic (like a messy room), what **fear of the unknown** might be hiding underneath that mask?
2. **The Non-Anxious Presence:** On a scale of 1 to 10, how well are you staying "emotionally separate" from your graduate's stress? Are you catching their anxiety, or are you acting as a stabilizer they can lean on?
3. **The Duality of Firsts and Lasts:** Which "final" event of senior year feels the heaviest for *you* personally? How can you acknowledge your own sense of loss while still leaving room for your graduate's unique emotional process?
4. **Wait for the Invite:** Can you recall a time recently when you gave advice that was heard as a "lecture"? How might that conversation have gone differently if you had asked, *"Would you like my perspective on that, or do you just need me to listen?"*
5. **The Adrenaline Crash:** Looking at your calendar for the week following graduation, is it packed with more activity, or have you scheduled "white space"? What is one low-stakes way your family can decompress together?
6. **The Discovery Phase:** If your graduate is struggling to find a summer job or a clear path, are you focusing on the "rearview mirror" (missed opportunities) or the "horizon"

(the next right step)? How can you model the belief that *"not knowing is not failing"*?

7. **Anticipatory Grief:** As your graduate's "Tribe" begins to shift, how are you making room for their new friends or social circles? Are you practicing hospitality to see their new world firsthand, or are you holding tight to the old one?
8. **The Brain in Progress:** How does knowing that the **prefrontal cortex** (the logic center) is still under construction change your expectations for your graduate's impulse control or "big picture" planning?
9. **The Consultant Mindset:** What is one "heavy load" your graduate is carrying right now that you can ask a curious question about, rather than trying to fix for them? (e.g., *"What feels like the biggest hurdle standing in your way today?"*)
10. **Your Own Emotional Gauge:** What is *your* "displacement behavior" when you feel the pressure of this transition? Do you get busier, withdraw, or become more controlling? Recognizing your own patterns is the first step to being a better coach.

### Looking Ahead: The Shift to Interdependence

You are now ready to move beyond the immediate logistics of the home to the lifelong philosophy of your new relationship. Chapter 6 explores the delicate balance of **Interdependence**—the stage where your graduate is no longer a dependent child, but not yet a fully autonomous peer. This is where the transition from "Manager" to "Mentor" becomes permanent.

We will unpack the psychological and conversational tools necessary to sustain this bond, including:

**Lifeguard vs. Life Coach:** A final, deep dive into the difference between *rescuing* (which disables) and *helping* (which empowers). We explore why a graduate who never stumbles never learns how to recover.

- **Safety Net vs. Hammock:** Defining the Boundaries of Your Support. You will learn how to provide the "Safety Net" that catches them during a true crisis without building a "Hammock" that stalls their maturity through perpetual comfort.
- **The "Golden Ratio" of Communication:** How to hit the professional standard of 43% talking and 57% listening, ensuring your graduate feels heard rather than managed.
- **The 3 Levels of Active Listening:** Moving from simply creating a safe environment to providing the "trampoline effect"—bouncing ideas back to help your graduate gain clarity on their own.
- **The Parent-Graduate Communication Agreement:** A formal framework for your "new rules of engagement," including the commitment to refrain from unsolicited advice and the "right to struggle."

# CHAPTER 6

## THE SHIFT TO INTERDEPENDENCE

A diploma is not a magic wand; it doesn't instantly bestow certainty, maturity, or self-assurance. For many graduates, the days following commencement feel less like a victory lap and more like standing at the rim of the Grand Canyon without a trail map.

While some young adults transition seamlessly into the workforce or higher education, others will hesitate, stumble, or change directions several times. Parents who expected a linear, predictable path often find themselves asking, "Did we miss something?" or "Why is this so much harder than we imagined?"

This is the critical juncture where the nature of parenting must evolve. It is the precise moment to shift your approach: moving away from the role of a **lifeguard**—constantly scanning for danger to intervene—and toward the role of a **life coach**, who guides from the sidelines as the graduate learns to navigate their own terrain.

### Lifeguard to Life Coaching

As introduced in Chapter Two, the transition from Lifeguard to Life Coach is a fundamental change in posture.

A **Lifeguard** jumps into the water to prevent failure at all costs. In contrast, a **Life Coach** stays close enough to provide guidance but far enough away to allow for growth. A graduate who never struggles never learns how to recover; a graduate who is rescued from every difficulty never learns the weight of responsibility.

Even in the post-graduate days, it is natural to want to fix what hurts your children—to call the employer, explain away the grade, or soften the consequences. However, adulthood is mastered through experience, not protection. Mistakes made after graduation are not proof of failure; they are evidence of development:

- **Losing a job** teaches accountability.
- **Dropping a class** teaches how to reassess priorities.
- **Choosing the wrong roommate** teaches discernment.

While these moments are painful, they are also formative. Parents who respond with calm curiosity and steady support teach something far more valuable than success: they teach resilience.

### Life Coaching Sounds Like:

- "What do you think you learned from this?"
- "What would you do differently next time?"
- "How can I support you without taking over?"

**It Does Not Sound Like:**

- "I told you so."
- "You're going to ruin your future."
- "Let me handle it for you."

There is a vital distinction between helping and rescuing. Helping empower, while rescuing disables. Helping asks questions;

rescuing removes consequences. Ultimately, helping builds confidence, while rescuing builds dependence.

### The Psychological Shift: **Relinquishing the Script**

The most difficult part of transitioning from Lifeguard to Life Coach is not the change in the graduate's behavior, but the change in the parent's heart. For two decades, your success as a parent was measured by your ability to provide a safe path; now, success is measured by your ability to let them navigate an unsafe one.

When we rescue our children, we are often managing our own anxiety rather than their problems. We step in because it is painful for us to watch them struggle. However, when you refuse to play the Lifeguard, you send a powerful, unspoken message to your graduate: "**I believe you are capable of handling this.**" That vote of confidence is the true fuel of adulthood.

### Safety Net vs **Hammock**

It is essential to clearly define the boundaries of your support. There is a profound difference between providing a **safety net** and offering a **hammock**.

- **The Safety Net:** For catastrophic failure. It is the support that prevents total destruction—health crises, true emergencies, or unforeseen disasters. A safety net is meant to catch someone so they can stand back up.
- **The Hammock:** This is support that allows for perpetual comfort at the expense of progress. When parents provide a "hammock"—paying for every luxury, resolving every minor debt, or doing the "adulting" tasks for them—they inadvertently stall the graduate's development.

Maturity is a byproduct of friction. By removing the friction, we unintentionally remove the growth.

. . .

**FROM DIRECTIVES to Discovery**

A Lifeguard gives orders; a Life Coach asks "Discovery Questions."

- **Directive:** "You need to go talk to your professor tomorrow morning."
- **Discovery:** "What do you think the next logical step is to get that grade back on track?"

The directive solves the immediate problem, but the discovery question builds the cognitive muscle they will need for the rest of their lives.

ARE YOU LISTENING OR TALKING?

In the professional arena, top-tier communicators often adhere to a "Golden Ratio," spending 43% of their time speaking and 57% listening. In the casual dynamics of parenting, however, conversations often dissolve into a "battle for airtime," where every remark feels like it requires an immediate response and silence is avoided at all costs.

Moving toward a more balanced communication style requires identifying where you land on the spectrum between "talker" and "listener." By reflecting on these behaviors, you can begin to shift toward that "Golden Ratio," ensuring your graduate feels heard rather than managed.

THE "GOLDEN RATIO" **in Practice**

Shifting your communication toward the 43/57 "Golden Ratio" requires more than just staying quiet; it requires active, curious listening. In the Life Coach model, your goal is to help the graduate find the solution within themselves rather than handing it to them on a platter.

. . .

### The Power of the "Pregnant Pause"

When your graduate shares a struggle—a difficult boss, a failed test, or a financial blunder—resist the urge to fill the silence with a solution. Often, the best coaching happens in the three seconds after they stop talking. That silence is an invitation for them to reflect, clarify, and eventually, take the lead in solving the problem.

### Parental Listening Self-Assessment

For each statement, honestly consider how often it describes your interactions with your children or family members:

- **The "Wait-Time" Test:** When your child finishes a sentence, do you pause for at least two seconds before responding, or do you jump in immediately to fill the silence?
- **The Response Strategy:** During a difficult conversation, are you mentally formulating your "rebuttal" or advice while they are still speaking?
- **The Question Quality:** Do you find yourself asking "Yes/No" questions (e.g., "Did you have a good day?"). Or do you use expansive prompts that encourage them to share more?
- **The Emotional Accuracy:** Can you summarize the emotion your child is feeling before you offer a solution to their problem?
- **The Distraction Factor:** Are you able to maintain consistent eye contact and minimize digital distractions while they are talking to you?

#### Interpreting Your Results

- **Mostly "Talker":** If you find yourself frequently jumping in or planning your response, you may be stuck in the "battle for airtime" mentioned earlier. You might be operating at the average 25% efficiency rate, where much of the message is missed.

- **The "Sponge" (Passive Listener):** You are quiet and observant, but you may not be providing the "trampoline" effect—bouncing ideas back to help your child gain clarity.
- **The "Trampoline" (Active Listener):** You are hitting that 57/43 listening-to-speaking ratio. You listen to understand, not just to respond, and your questions help the speaker feel truly supported

## The 3 Levels of Active Listening

Effective listening can be broken down into these progressive stages:

**Level 1: The Safe Environment**

Goal: Make the graduate feel safe to express complex or emotional thoughts.

Action: Minimize distractions and use non-verbal cues (nodding, eye contact) to show you are present.

**Level 2: The Clearinghouse**

Goal: Remove your own biases and internal "rebuttal" dialogue.

Action: Practice "wait-time." Instead of jumping in the second, they pause, wait two seconds to ensure they have finished their thought.

**Level 3: The Collaborative Loop**

Goal: Help the graduate gain more clarity than they had before they started talking.

Action: Ask open-ended questions rather than "yes/no" questions.

## High-Value Questions to Ask

To practice Level 3 listening, try using these prompts instead of offering immediate advice:

- *"What do you think is the biggest hurdle in this situation?"*
- *"How did that experience change your perspective on [Topic]?"*
- *"It sounds like you're feeling [Emotion] because of [Situation]—is that right?"*

**THE PARENT-GRADUATE COMMUNICATION Agreement**

The transition from "Manager" to "Mentor" is often smoother when the new rules of engagement are clearly defined. Below is a framework for an agreement that honors the graduate's growing independence while maintaining the parent's role as a source of wisdom.

**1. The Strategy of "The Ask"**

The Commitment: Parents agree to refrain from offering unsolicited advice.

The Action:

Unless a situation involves immediate physical safety or a violation of pre-set "House Rules," parents will wait for the graduate to ask for a "coaching perspective" before providing a solution.

The Phrase:

"Are you looking for a listening ear, or would you like my input as a coach on this one?"

**2. The Golden Ratio of Communication**

The Commitment: Both parties strive for a 43/57 talking-to-listening ratio.

The Action:

Practice the "three-second pause" after the other person finishes speaking. This ensures the speaker feels fully heard and prevents the conversation from feeling like a "battle for airtime."

**3. Defining the Safety Net vs. the Hammock**

The Commitment: Distinguish between support that catches (Safety Net) and support that coddles (Hammock).

Safety Net: Emergency health issues, car breakdowns on the highway, or major life crises.

Hammock: Administrative tasks (scheduling appointments), minor financial oversights due to lack of planning, or resolving interpersonal conflicts with bosses or roommates.

**4. The Discovery Zone**

The Commitment: We replace directives with discovery questions.

The Action:

Instead of saying "You should do X," parents will ask, "What are the three options you see for resolving this?" This builds the graduate's "decision-making muscle."

**5. Scheduled Check-ins vs. Constant Surveillance**

The Commitment: Moving away from "tracking" and toward "connecting."

The Action:

Rather than daily "status updates" on chores or job applications, we agree to a weekly or bi-weekly "Life Update" that focuses on relationships and high-level goals rather than a checklist of tasks.

**6. The Right to Struggle**

The Commitment: We acknowledge that friction is a requirement for growth.

The Action:

Parents give the graduate permission to be frustrated or to fail at a task without immediately jumping in to "save the day." Graduates agree to view these moments as learning opportunities rather than signs of abandonment.

## Reflection Questions for the Agreement

1. Which part of this agreement feels the most "dangerous" to you as a parent? Why?
2. How would your relationship change if "The Ask" became the standard for all advice-giving?
3. Are there specific "Hammock" behaviors you are currently

providing that need to be transitioned into "Safety Net" boundaries?

4. How can you communicate this agreement to your graduate as a vote of confidence in their ability rather than a withdrawal of your love?

### The Goal: **Interdependence, Not Independence**

The ultimate aim of the Life Coach is not to create a child who never needs their parents again. The goal is **interdependence.**

Independence is the ability to stand alone; interdependence is the ability for two healthy, capable adults to stand together. By stepping back from the role of Lifeguard, you are clearing the way for a new, adult relationship to form—one built on mutual respect, shared wisdom, and a bond that no longer relies on control, but on choice.

### Emotional Swings

Parents should expect emotional swings during this season. A graduate may feel entirely capable one week and completely overwhelmed the next. While independence is exciting, it is also exhausting; learning to manage time, finances, relationships, and professional responsibilities simultaneously is heavy work.

When disappointment inevitably comes, the natural parental temptation is to panic. However, panic often leads to control, control leads to conflict, and conflict creates distance.

**Connection** is what keeps your influence alive. Staying connected does not require you to solve every problem; it simply requires being present. Parents who choose the right timing, speak with calm voices, and listen without interrupting preserve trust—even when the conversations are difficult. Influence is protected only when the relationship is protected.

Discerning what to say—and, more importantly, what **not** to say—is the definitive sign that a parent is embracing the role of Life

Coach. Graduates who feel respected are far more likely to seek guidance on their own. Conversely, those who feel judged are more likely to hide their struggles. By listening without panic, you become a safe harbor for honest conversation and a steady anchor for their growth.

### Stepping Back

Some parents fear that stepping back is the same as stepping away. In reality, stepping back creates the necessary space for maturity to take root. The goal is not to withdraw your love, but to shift your posture—moving from director to advisor, and from manager to mentor.

Graduates need the assurance that they are not alone, but they also need the dignity of knowing that their lives belong to them. This season is not defined by perfection; it is defined by progress. Parents who can say, "We will walk with you, but we will not walk for *you*," provide their graduates with a dual gift: the security of support and the dignity of strength.

When the road feels especially unclear, families often discover a vital truth: they were never intended to navigate this journey in isolation.

### Building a Support Network

As families navigate this transitional phase, it's crucial to recognize the power of community. Friends, mentors, and fellow graduates can provide invaluable support. Sharing experiences can alleviate feelings of isolation and foster a sense of belonging. Graduates often find comfort in knowing that others face similar challenges, reinforcing the idea that they are not alone in their struggles.

**Encourage your graduate to seek out connections:**

- Peer Support Groups: Many colleges and organizations offer groups where students can share their experiences and challenges.

- Mentorship Programs: Connecting with someone who has successfully navigated the path can provide guidance and encouragement.
- Family Connections: Extended family members can also serve as mentors, sharing their own life lessons and insights.

### Embracing Uncertainty

Uncertainty can be daunting, but it also opens doors to unexpected opportunities. Encourage graduates to view setbacks as detours rather than dead ends. Each twist and turn can lead to new insights and paths.

- Reflect and Adapt: Teach graduates to reflect on their experiences. What did they learn from a setback? How can they apply those lessons moving forward?
- Stay Open-Minded: Encourage them to remain open to new possibilities, even if they differ from their original plans. Life often unfolds in surprising ways.

### Celebrating Small Wins

Amid the chaos of change, it's essential to celebrate progress, no matter how small. Recognizing achievements can boost confidence and motivation.

- Set Achievable Goals: Help your graduate set realistic, short-term goals that lead to a sense of accomplishment.
- Celebrate Efforts: Acknowledge both the effort and the outcome. Whether it's completing a project, making a new friend, or learning a new skill, every step forward deserves recognition.

. . .

### Encouraging a Growth Mindset

Fostering a growth mindset can empower graduates to face challenges with resilience. Teach them to embrace failure as a stepping stone to success.

- Language Matters: Encourage positive self-talk and reframing negative thoughts. Instead of saying, "I failed," encourage them to say, "I learned something valuable."
- Focus on the Journey: Remind them that personal growth is a lifelong process, and every experience contributes to their development.

### Not a Straight Line

In the face of uncertainty and setbacks, the journey toward adulthood becomes a canvas for profound growth. Parents who embrace this transition as an invitation for partnership—rather than an exercise in control—empower their graduates to forge their own paths with genuine confidence.

Ultimately, the road beyond graduation is rarely a straight line; it is a winding path defined by both peaks and valleys. By providing steady guidance without reaching for the steering wheel, you help your graduate navigate their unique journey with resilience and internal strength. In doing so, you move toward a family culture rooted in trust and open communication, where challenges are no longer seen as crises to be managed, but as opportunities for deeper connection.

As the dust settles and new horizons emerge, remember: the journey is just beginning. Every step—whether it feels like a stride forward or a stumble backward—carries the invaluable lessons that will shape the person they are becoming.

PARENT REFLECTION QUESTIONS:

1. **Rescuing vs. Helping:** Can you identify a recent moment where you "jumped into the water" to solve a problem for your graduate? Looking back, did your intervention build their **confidence** or their **dependence**?
2. **The Heart of the Coach:** When you feel the urge to rescue your child from a struggle, is it because *they* can't handle the situation, or because *you* can't handle the anxiety of watching them fail?
3. **Safety Net vs. Hammock:** Take an honest audit of your current support. Are you providing a **Safety Net** (meant to catch them so they can stand back up) or a **Hammock** (allowing for comfort at the expense of progress)? What is one "hammock" luxury you can begin to phase out?
4. **The "Golden Ratio" Challenge:** In your next "Life Update" conversation, try to hit the 43/57 ratio. Can you commit to listening more than you speak? What is the hardest part about staying quiet for you?
5. **The Power of the Pause:** The next time your graduate presents a problem, can you wait **three full seconds** after they finish talking before you respond? What do you think they might say in that silence if given the space?
6. **Discovery over Directives:** Think of a piece of advice you've been dying to give. How can you rephrase that "Directive" (You should...) into a "**Discovery Question**" (What do you think the next step is...)?
7. **The Right to Struggle:** Do you truly believe that "friction is a requirement for growth"? If so, how can you communicate to your graduate that your stepping back is a **vote of confidence** in their strength, not a withdrawal of your love?

8. **Interdependence vs. Independence:** How do you define a successful adult relationship with your child? Is it them never needing you, or is it two healthy adults choosing to stand together? How does that shift your daily interactions?
9. **The "Invite" Protocol:** How would your relationship change if you committed to "The Ask"—waiting for them to ask for your coaching perspective before giving it? Are you willing to risk them making a mistake in order to protect that boundary?
10. **The Anchor of Connection:** When the inevitable "emotional swings" happen, are you focusing more on the **problem** (the job, the grade, the breakup) or the **connection**? How can you remain a "safe harbor" even when you disagree with their choices?

LOOKING AHEAD: **Letting Go Without Letting Down**

The final movement of this transition is perhaps the most difficult for the parent's heart: learning to loosen the grip without losing the connection. Chapter 7, **Letting Go Without Letting Down**, explores the shift from authority to influence. It is the moment you officially trade your "Manager" title for that of a "Mentor," recognizing that while your volume may soften, the weight of your voice actually increases when it is rooted in respect rather than control.

In this concluding section, we will cover:

- **The Transfer of Title:** Identifying the five key areas—finances, schedule, relationships, faith, and career—that now belong entirely to the graduate.
- **Connection by Invitation:** Why "How are you doing?" must replace "What are you doing?" to keep the lines of communication open in an adult relationship.

- **Weathering the Inconsistency:** Learning to tolerate the "messy" stages of growth, understanding that a graduate's withdrawal or rejection of advice is often a symptom of development, not a rejection of you.
- **Redefining the Win:** Shifting your definition of success from "Grade Points" (performance) to "Character Points" (resilience and wisdom).
- **The Power of Presence:** How to stay emotionally available without hovering, ensuring your graduate knows you are a "safe harbor" they can return to by choice, not by mandate.

This chapter serves as the ultimate vote of confidence. By letting go, you aren't stepping away; you are stepping into a new, lifelong partnership. You are giving your graduate the freedom to build their own life and the security of knowing you are walking beside them as they do.

# CHAPTER 7

## LETTING GO WITHOUT LETTING DOWN

One of the most difficult lessons for parents in this season is learning how to loosen the grip without losing influence. Letting go does not mean stepping aside emotionally; it means changing the way we hold on.

For years, parents have functioned as managers—organizing schedules, enforcing rules, and solving problems. This role was vital during the formative years, but after graduation, management must give way to mentoring. Control gives way to connection, and direction yields to dialogue.

### Trading Control for Trust

Many parents fear that releasing control will lead to immediate chaos. In reality, holding too tightly often creates the very resistance we hope to avoid. Young adults who feel controlled tend to pull away, while those who feel trusted are more likely to lean in. This fear of chaos often stems from a deep desire to protect, but it can inadvertently create barriers to the very communication and trust we need to maintain.

. . .

### The Transfer of Title: **Whose Life Is It?**

Letting go begins with recognizing what now belongs to the graduate. Decisions regarding finances, schedules, friendships, faith involvement, and career direction are no longer assignments to be approved; they are responsibilities to be mastered. Parents can still offer guidance and insight, but they must do so with humility rather than authority.

This shift does not mean you stop caring; it means you care differently. Adapting to this new dynamic allows you to find effective ways to show support without overstepping the necessary boundaries of adulthood.

### Connection by Invitation

Staying emotionally connected requires intentional effort. When children were young, connections happened naturally through proximity. Now, it happens through invitation. Parents must create a space where conversation feels safe, curiosity is genuine, and vulnerability is welcomed.

Connection grows when parents ask more than they tell:

- **"How are you doing?"** matters more than **"What are you doing?"**
- **"What do you think?"** matters more than **"Here's what you should do."**

Listening communicates respect. Respect builds trust. Trust keeps the relationship alive.

### Low-Pressure Rhythms

Parents may need to initiate connection in creative ways—inviting a graduate to coffee, sending a simple text of encouragement, or taking a walk together rather than sitting face-to-face. These small acts signal availability without pressure. The goal is to foster an environment where open dialogue is encouraged, never forced.

- **Shared Activities:** Engaging in hobbies you both enjoy creates natural opportunities for conversation.
- **Open-Ended Questions:** Use prompts that require more than a "yes" or "no" to encourage deeper discussion.
- **Low-Pressure Check-Ins:** Regular, brief points of contact help maintain the bond over time.

### WEATHERING the Inconsistency

Emotional connection requires a high level of patience. Graduates will not always communicate with clarity; some will withdraw, while others will overshare. They may seek advice one day and reject it the next. This inconsistency is not a rejection of you; it is a symptom of their development.

Parents must learn to tolerate discomfort without rushing to reclaim control. Silence does not always mean distance, and struggle does not always mean failure. Growth often looks messy before it achieves maturity.

### FROM GRADE POINT to Character Point

One of the most important tasks of this season is redefining success. It is no longer measured by report cards, trophies, or adherence to your schedule. Instead, it is measured by character, responsibility, and resilience.

A successful season is not one where everything goes smoothly; it is one in which a graduate learns to navigate difficulty without quitting or hiding.

- A lost job teaches **perseverance.**
- A challenging class teaches **discipline.**

- A failed relationship teaches **wisdom**

Parents who redefine success stop asking, "Is my child doing everything right?" and start asking, **"Is my child learning to live wisely?"**

### The Discovery Model: Asking vs. Telling

Letting go without letting down means staying present without hovering. It means being available without being intrusive.

A helpful way to frame this shift is:

- **Monitoring asks:** "Did you do what I said?"
- **Mentoring asks:** "What did you learn from that?"

Graduates who know their parents are emotionally available but not controlling are far more likely to return for counsel. They come back not because they must, but because they trust.

### The Power of Presence Over Authority

Parents often worry that if they step back, they will become unnecessary. In truth, the opposite often happens: influence grows when authority fades. Your voice gains weight when your volume softens. This season calls for a different kind of strength—the strength to release without retreating and to guide without gripping.

- **Empathy:** Understanding the unique challenges your graduate faces helps your support resonate more effectively.
- **Encouragement:** Celebrating small victories reinforces their sense of achievement.
- **Flexibility:** Being open to changing your approach as your graduate's needs evolve.

. . .

**The Ultimate Vote of Confidence**

Letting go is not abandonment; it is an act of belief. It is the belief that the foundation you built still stands. It is the belief that your graduate has the capacity to grow. The belief is that connection matters more than control.

Parents who learn to let go without letting down give their graduates two priceless gifts: the freedom to become who they were meant to be, and a relationship strong enough to walk with them while they do.

~

## Parent Reflection Questions:

To help you process the final transition from management to mentorship, use these ten reflection questions. They are designed to help you examine the "grip" you have on your graduate's life and pivot toward a relationship built on mutual respect and choice.

1. **Changing the Grip:** If "letting go" isn't stepping away, but rather *changing the way you hold on*, how would you describe your current hold? Is it a tight grip of control or a supportive, open hand?
2. **The Fear of Chaos:** Be honest with yourself—what is the specific "chaos" you are most afraid will happen if you release control of your graduate's schedule or finances? Is that fear based on their current ability or your own need to protect?
3. **The Transfer of Title:** Look at the five key areas: finances, schedules, friendships, faith, and career. Which of these is the hardest for you to "hand over the title" to? Why does that specific area feel so high-stakes for you?

4. **Connection by Invitation:** When was the last time you waited for an *invitation* to connect rather than initiating through proximity or "checking in" on a task? How can you create a "safe space" this week that signals you are available but not intrusive?
5. **The "What" vs. the "How":** In your recent conversations, have you focused more on *what* they are doing (tasks/logistics) or *how* they are doing (emotions/character)? How can you pivot your next talk toward the "heart rate" of their life?
6. **Tolerating Inconsistency:** When your graduate is inconsistent—seeking advice one day and rejecting it the next—do you take it personally? How can you remind yourself that this "messiness" is a symptom of their growth, not a rejection of your wisdom?
7. **Redefining the Win:** If success is no longer about "Grade Points" (doing things right), but "Character Points" (learning to live wisely), what is one "successful" struggle your graduate has navigated recently?
8. **Monitoring vs. Mentoring:** Think of a question you plan to ask them today. Does it sound like a monitor ("Did you do what I said?") or a mentor ("What did you learn from that experience?")?
9. **The Weight of Your Voice:** Can you identify a moment where your influence actually grew because you softened your volume or stepped back from your authority? What did that look like?
10. **The Ultimate Vote of Confidence:** If letting go is an "act of belief," what is one specific thing you truly believe about your graduate's character or resilience that gives you the courage to let them lead their own life?

**LOOKING AHEAD: What SAT Scores Don't Tell You**

Standardized tests like the SAT and ACT are often treated as the final word on a student's future, but they remain silent on the qualities that truly sustain a successful life. Chapter 8, **What SAT Scores Don't Tell You**, shifts the focus from academic benchmarks to the essential balance between "Hard Skills" and "Soft Skills." While hard skills might get a graduate through the door, it is their soft skills—emotional intelligence, resilience, and adaptability—that will keep them in the room.

In the upcoming chapter, we will explore:

- **The Incomplete Map:** Why testing results are often skewed by anxiety or access to resources, and why they fail to measure a graduate's readiness for real-world complexity.
- **The Hard vs. Soft Skill Audit:** A breakdown of technical competencies (Hard Skills) versus the character traits (Soft Skills) that function as the "pulse" of maturity.
- **The Personality and Soft Skills Assessment:** A practical tool designed for both the parent and graduate to complete separately. This exercise surfaces hidden gaps in perception and turns "generalized worry" into a focused action plan.
- **The Soft Skills Growth Plan:** A roadmap for moving a skill from "Developing" to "Proficient" using micro-habits, identifying friction points, and establishing a "Life Coach" partnership.
- **A Final Benediction:** A reminder that a score is a snapshot, not a sentence. By focusing on character and resilience, you are equipping your graduate with a toolkit that will serve them long after their test scores have been forgotten.

This chapter is designed to move your conversations away from the pressure of performance and toward the beauty of preparation, ensuring your graduate is ready for the unpredictable journey of a well-lived life.

# CHAPTER 8

## BEYOND THE TEST SCORES

Although SAT and ACT scores are widely regarded as the definitive benchmark for college readiness, they only capture a narrow glimpse of a student's true potential. These standardized tests evaluate specific cognitive abilities, such as mathematical reasoning and verbal proficiency, but they remain silent on the essential qualities that sustain a meaningful life: creativity, emotional intelligence, practical problem-solving, and character.

Standardized results often provide an incomplete map of a graduate's readiness for the complexities of the real world. A high score may be inflated by access to test-prep resources, while a low score may simply be the byproduct of test anxiety. To see the full picture of a student's future success, we must shift our focus toward the critical balance between "Hard Skills" and "Soft Skills."

### Assessing Readiness: Hard Skills

As seniors transition from the structured classroom to the ambiguity of adulthood, evaluating hard skills remains essential. These are the specific, teachable, and measurable abilities required for technical competency.

- **Academic Knowledge:** Mastery of core concepts in math, science, and language.
- **Technical Proficiency:** Skill with productivity software, coding, or specific trade tools.
- **Certifications:** Tangible credentials such as CPR, a driver's license, or vocational certifications.

These skills are often the "entry ticket" to a career or degree program, easily assessed through portfolios, transcripts, and practical tests.

### Assessing Readiness: Soft Skills

Equally vital—and often more predictive of long-term success—are soft skills. These are the interpersonal attributes and character traits that allow a person to navigate the "friction" of life. Communication, teamwork, adaptability, and emotional maturity are the engines of a successful career and a healthy home.

While soft skills are harder to quantify, they are the "pulse" of a graduate's maturity. They are observed in how a graduate handles a conflict with a roommate, manages a difficult boss, or stays resilient after a rejection letter.

### Using the Assessment

By combining hard- and soft-skill evaluations, parents and graduates can move away from "generalized worry" toward a focused action plan. This integrated view allows you to:

- Identify technical gaps that need a specific course or workshop.
- Encourage group activities or mentoring to strengthen interpersonal deficits.
- Pursue real-world experiences that build the "resilience muscle."

As a Life Coach, your goal is to support this assessment process while encouraging the graduate's autonomy, ensuring they take the lead in their own development.

~

**Personality and Soft Skills Assessment Tool**

This tool is designed to surface insights about habits and tendencies that testing alone will never reveal.

**A Gentle Warning:** Ideally, the parent and the graduate should complete this assessment separately, then compare their results. This comparison often prompts honest—and sometimes challenging—conversations.

Approach the "Compare and Contrast" session with truthfulness and kindness. The goal is a deeper understanding and constructive planning, not judgment.

**Instructions**

1. Read each statement carefully.
2. Rate the graduate on a scale from 1-5

1 - Strongly Disagree
2 - Disagree
3 - Neutral
4 - Agree
5 - Strongly Agree

Assessment Questions

**A. Communication Skills**

___Expresses thoughts clearly and effectively in writing and speech.

___Practices active listening and responds appropriately rather than just waiting to speak.

**B. Teamwork and Collaboration**

___Works well in groups and values others' contributions.

___Is willing to compromise to achieve a common group goal.

**C. Adaptability and Flexibility**

___Adjusts plans and strategies when unexpected challenges arise.

___Embraces change as an opportunity for growth rather than a crisis.

**D. Problem-Solving Skills**

___Analyzes problems logically to develop effective solutions.

___Remains calm and focused in high-pressure situations.

**E. Emotional Intelligence**

___Is aware of personal emotions and manages them effectively.

___Shows empathy and seeks to understand others' feelings.

**F. Time Management**

___Prioritizes tasks effectively and consistently meets deadlines.

___Balances multiple responsibilities (work, school, social) without becoming overwhelmed.

**G. Leadership Qualities**

___ Comfortable taking initiative and guiding others when a "gap" exists.

___Encourages and motivates peers to achieve their best.

**H. Conflict Resolution**

___Handles disagreements in a constructive, non-combative manner.

___Seeks to understand both sides of an argument before forming a conclusion.

**Scoring and Interpretation**

**Total your scores (16–80 possible points)**

The ultimate purpose of this exercise is to talk about strengths and areas underdeveloped. Use this general scoring range as a starter for discussion on developing a soft skills growth plan.

**16–49: Developing** – This area needs intentional focus. Consider workshops, volunteer roles, or specific practical experiences to build these muscles.

**50-64: Competent** – There is a solid foundation here. Continued practice and real-world "friction" will further strengthen these abilities.

**65–80: Proficient** – These are primary strengths. Look for leadership roles or academic pursuits that leverage these high-level skills.

NEXT STEPS: **Moving Toward Interdependence**

**Reflection:** Where did the graduate's self-score differ most from the parent's score? Why is there a gap in perception?

**Action Plan:** Choose **one** soft skill from the "Developing" or "Competent" range. What is one specific, real-world goal the graduate can set this month to improve that skill?

### Soft Skills Growth Plan

THIS PLAN IS DESIGNED to help the graduate move a specific skill from "Developing" to "Proficient" through intentional, real-world practice.

SKILL FOCUS______________________________

*(Example: Time Management, Conflict Resolution, or Problem-Solving)*

**The "Why" (The Motivation)**

How will mastering this skill make your life easier or more successful in the next six months?

**The "Micro-Habit" (The Action)**

What is **one** small, repeatable action you will take this week to practice this skill?

**Instead of:** "I'll be more organized."

**Try:** "I will use a digital calendar to track all deadlines and appointments."

**The "Friction" Point (The Challenge)**

What is the biggest obstacle that usually stops you from using this skill? (e.g., procrastination, fear of difficult conversations, or physical distractions).

~

### The "Life Coach" Support (The Partnership)

**Parents' Commitment:**

I will support this growth by...

[ ] Refraining from giving reminders.

[ ] Being available for a "Discovery"conversation if you get stuck.

[ ] Celebrating when I see you take the lead.

**Other:** ______________________________

### The 30-Day Milestone

How will we know this skill is growing?

*Example: "I will have successfully managed my own budget for four consecutive weeks."*

~

### A Chapter Benediction

As you close this chapter on assessment, remember that a score is a snapshot, not a sentence. The value of this exercise isn't the number on the page; it is the conversation it sparks between parent and graduate.

By focusing on the "Soft Skills" of character and resilience, you are giving your graduate a toolkit that will serve them long after their SAT scores have been forgotten. You aren't just preparing them for a test; you are preparing them for the beautiful, unpredictable journey of a well-lived life.

**Parent Reflection Questions:**

**Beyond the Numbers:** When you look at your graduate's standardized test scores or GPA, does it evoke a sense of pride, anxiety, or relief? How much of that emotion is tied to their actual readiness for life versus your own desire for academic validation?

1. **The "Full Picture" Audit:** Think of a time your graduate faced a real-world problem (a car breakdown, a scheduling conflict, or a social misunderstanding). Which **Soft Skill** did they use to navigate it, and how did that skill serve them better than any "Hard Skill" could have in that moment?
2. **The Gap in Perception:** If you and your graduate complete the assessment separately and find a significant gap in a specific score (e.g., they rate themselves a "5" in Time Management and you rate them a "2"), how will you approach that conversation without becoming the "Prosecutor"?
3. **Inflation vs. Anxiety:** Consider the "Hard Skills" listed (Academic Knowledge, Technical Proficiency). Are there areas where your graduate's performance has been hindered by anxiety rather than a lack of ability? How can you coach the heart behind the skill?
4. **The Engine of Success:** Which of the eight soft skills listed in the assessment do you believe is the most critical "engine" for your graduate's chosen path? Why do you value that specific trait above the others?
5. **Micro-Habits vs. Grand Gestures:** In the **Soft Skills Growth Plan**, we focus on "Micro-Habits." Why is a small, repeatable action (like using a digital calendar) more

valuable for a launching adult than a grand promise to "be better"?

6. **The Life Coach's Commitment:** Looking at the support options (refraining from reminders, being available for discovery, and celebrating leadership), which one is the most difficult for you to commit to? What does that reveal about your own "Lifeguard" tendencies?
7. **Redefining Failure:** How can you reframe a low score in a "Developing" skill as an opportunity for **intentional growth** rather than a character flaw? How can you communicate this to your graduate as a "training camp" moment?
8. **The Resilience Muscle:** What is one "real-world friction" point your graduate is currently facing? Instead of smoothing it over, how can you use the assessment tool to help them see it as a chance to build their resilience?
9. **The Snapshot vs. The Sentence:** As you look toward the next 30 days, how will you ensure that the results of this assessment remain a "snapshot" of where they are today, rather than a "sentence" defining who they will be tomorrow?

### Looking Ahead: The God Factor

The previous chapters have provided a roadmap for managing logistics, budgets, and the transition from hard skills to soft skills. However, as every parent eventually discovers, there is a limit to human preparation. Chapter 9, **The God Factor**, addresses the moment when your child moves beyond the reach of your hands and into a season where faith becomes the primary anchor for both the parent and the graduate.

In the upcoming chapter, we will explore:

- **Relinquishing the Illusion of Control:** An honest look at the "Physical Distance" that high school graduation creates —and why this shift is not a dead end, but an invitation to step into a deeper faith.
- **The Three Pillars of a Sustained Life:** A breakdown of the Physical, Emotional, and Spiritual foundations necessary to carry a person through the inevitable complexities and weight of a long life.
- **The "Parental Safety" Myth:** Why trusting God does not mean abandoning responsibility, but rather releasing the heavy (and impossible) burden of trying to be the sole author of your child's safety.
- **A Legacy of Providence:** Real-world stories from the Seago family—from the front lines of Afghanistan to late-night drives and city streets—demonstrating that while Mom and Dad were miles away, God was nearby.
- **The Hand-Off:** Understanding the "Journey of Faith and Discovery," where a graduate begins to transition from a "borrowed" family tradition to an "owned" personal conviction through honest inquiry and reflection.
- **The Spiritual Mentor Shift:** How to move from the one providing all the answers to becoming a prayerful advocate—the "voice in the stands" cheering them on as they discover their own calling.

THIS CHAPTER IS DESIGNED to move your heart from a state of "Lifeguard" anxiety to the peace of a "Life Coach," anchoring your hope in a foundation that will not collapse when life's storms inevitable arrive.

# CHAPTER 9

## THE GOD FACTOR

If this book is in your hands, you already feel the heavy responsibility of raising a child. Whether your family is large or small, you've seen countless moments of grace and providence. For years, you've tended the daily details—setting boundaries, keeping them safe, and offering steady, ongoing guidance.

Then come the milestones: a driver's license, a graduation cap, a move to a college dorm, a first apartment, or a military base. These moments create a physical distance we can no longer bridge, and the daily oversight that once defined our lives suddenly becomes impossible. It is natural to feel a sense of helplessness in this transition, but that shift isn't a dead end—it is an invitation.

Relinquishing control isn't about stepping away; it is about stepping into a deeper faith. It is the realization that the same God who witnessed their first breath is the same God watching over them in the places we cannot go. When we reach the limits of our reach, we find peace in knowing they are never out of His sight.

### The Foundation of Our Story

For the Seagos, faith has been the bedrock of our home—the

primary lens through which we have navigated over forty years of parenting. It is a perspective woven into every chapter of our lives, yet we recognize that every family builds their foundation in a unique way.

If faith is not your primary focus, we truly respect the diverse beliefs and values that guide your household. However, if you are open to hearing how our convictions made this journey possible, we invite you to explore this chapter. Our hope is that these lessons offer a sense of encouragement and peace as you walk your own path.

## THE ARCHITECT and the Creator

Even in homes where formal religious practice isn't part of the daily rhythm, families still communicate a set of values. Often, these are rooted in a philosophy of self-determination—the idea that we are the primary architects of our own lives.

We see this reflected in the way we encourage our graduates to "seize the day," take charge of their destinies, and rely on their own strength to achieve success. Whether your guidance is rooted in a personal philosophy of self-reliance or a deep spiritual tradition, the transition from high school to adulthood remains a sacred threshold for us all.

## THE THREE PILLARS of a Sustained Life

While that drive for independence is admirable, self-reliance alone isn't always enough to carry a person through the inevitable weight and complexity of a long life. We believe every human experience is supported by three essential pillars:

- **The Physical:** Our health and our tangible presence in the world.
- **The Emotional:** Our internal landscape and the depth of our relationships.

- **The Spiritual:** The deeper sense of meaning and purpose that sustains us when the first two pillars are tested.

Ultimately, it is a person's faith—that quiet, steady trust in something greater than themselves—that serves as the engine for their spiritual foundation. It provides a strength that goes far beyond simple willpower, offering a "peace that passes understanding" during life's greatest transitions.

### Surrendering the Illusion of Control

There comes a point in every parent's life when we must admit: *"I cannot be God in all places at all times."* Deep love often convinces us that if we watch closely enough, warn loudly enough, or plan carefully enough, we can shield our children from every harm. We manage schedules, monitor relationships, and calculate risks as if control were the same thing as care.

However, trusting God does not mean we abandon our responsibility; it means we release the illusion that we alone are the authors of our children's safety.

### Leaning on Greater Protection

In the final season of a graduate's life at home, there are moments when hope and faith are the only tools left in the toolkit. We pray daily for their safety, for the right influences to cross their paths, and for wisdom to take root in their hearts during critical moments.

Parents who dedicate their children shortly after birth often acknowledge this reality early on: our power is limited. We choose to partner with God in the raising of a child—a form of spiritual co-parenting. While we handle the daily tasks of meals, guidance, and late-night conversations, we learn to let God carry the greater burden of guarding their fragile lives and their future steps.

We realized how fragile our children were as they began their journeys into adult life after graduation.

. . .

KATES'S LATE **Nights**

Now a mother of two, Health Policy Government Affairs Consultant

Kate was known for her vibrant, energetic personality and a record of academic achievement that set a strong foundation for her transition into adulthood. Her college years were marked by significant hard work, requiring grit to balance demanding studies with late-night shifts in the restaurant industry. Practical challenges, such as unreliable vehicles, were common during this period. It was a time of making do with what was available—reflecting the family's shared resilience as she pursued higher education.

In an era before cell phones, the lack of instant communication added a quiet tension to those long nights. The simple sight of headlights turning into the driveway became the greatest relief of the day —a silent reassurance of safety and a successful return home. This nightly ritual underscored the deep connection and relief felt when a child finally navigated the day's hurdles. These moments of arrival signified more than the end of a work shift; they served as a testament to a family's resilience and to the steady character formed in children during the early season of life coaching.

**Mom and Dad were miles away, but God was nearby. In our absence, He was present.**

WHERE'S CHARLA?

*Now a head coach for a fitness firm*

Charla's post–high school years ushered in a whirlwind of independence and determination as she balanced pursuing a degree, earning an income, and nurturing a relationship. In a household where attention was primarily devoted to her five younger siblings, her parents were less involved in the details of her daily life. One of our most memorable—and now laughable—moments occurred when Charla returned home after everyone was asleep, accidentally triggered the alarm system, and a fiercely protective dad charged down the stairs with a baseball bat, ready to defend his family from what he thought was an intruder.

Much like with her older sister, keeping track of Charla's whereabouts and schedule became an act of faith, best entrusted to prayer. Those stressful yet rewarding days of learning to be independent while remaining connected truly stretched—and ultimately strengthened—the family's prayer life.

**Mom and Dad were miles away, but God was nearby. In our absence, He was present.**

### Rachelle's Guardian Angel

*Now a mother of six, grandmother of one, and business owner*

Rachelle had always been a natural leader, independent and determined to succeed in the competitive world of professional acting. This path required frequent late-night drives to Houston for rehearsals.

On one such evening, she pulled over at a gas station to check in with us. While at the payphone, she was jumped by three men; the struggle was violent enough that she was thrown to the ground and her dress ripped.

Just as the situation turned dire, a woman appeared from the station, her shouts driving the assailants away. A few days later, her father returned to the store to thank the woman who had come to his daughter's aid. But the staff was baffled. According to their records and memory, only male attendants had worked that shift, leaving the identity of Rachelle's guardian a complete mystery.

**Mom and Dad were miles away, but God was nearby. In our absence, He was present.**

### Nikki's Assault

*Now, a mother of four and private school owner*

Nikki was the heartbeat of our family, radiating a joy that lit up every room she entered. During her college years, she moved to a campus roughly 50 miles from home, where apartment life perfectly suited her independent spirit. Her place was a hub of activity, with friends always coming and going.

Even while spending her teenage years living in a gated community, Nikki possessed a natural level of street smarts. This inherent intuition served as a vital layer of protection, proving that her awareness wasn't dependent on her environment, but was a part of her own self-reliance.

That sense of security was challenged one evening when she stepped out after dark to pick up snacks for her roommates. As she approached her car, an assailant intercepted her, attempting to steal her purse. Showing remarkable presence of mind, she surrendered the bag to de-escalate the conflict and, thankfully, escaped the encounter unharmed.

**Mom and Dad were miles away, but God was nearby. In our absence, He was present.**

### John's Fight for a Car

*Now a father of two and president of a non-profit*

Responsibility had always been John's hallmark, so we celebrated his high school graduation by gifting him a car he truly cherished. However, that gift became a flashpoint of danger one night at a gas pump.

Confronted by a hooded man demanding cash, John found himself in the middle of a violent escalation. As the thief attempted to seize the car, John fought back, exchanging punches and physically dragging the man from the driver's seat.

Though the assailant ultimately fled, the cost could have been catastrophic. It was a terrifying reminder of how quickly a "well-done" gift could turn into a life-threatening encounter.

**Mom and Dad were miles away, but God was nearby. In our absence, He was present.**

. . .

### Scott in Afghanistan

*Now a father of four and a gifted mechanic*

Following high school graduation, Scott faced a period of uncertainty as he searched for his next step. That search eventually led him to the Marine Corps, where he traded his post-graduation indecision for the clear direction and discipline of a soldier. But the pride we felt watching him graduate boot camp was soon tempered by the gravity of his deployment.

Scott's first year in the Marine Corps took him to the front lines of Afghanistan, where he assisted in harrowing sniper-clearing operations. Living in a constant state of vulnerability, his frequent close calls in that dangerous territory brought a sharp clarity to his new life.

It was a period that moved him beyond the safety of our reach, marking the radical shift from the boy we knew to the soldier he had become. No longer sheltered by our protection or the routines of home, Scott was thrust into an environment where every decision carried weight and every day demanded courage. The distance—both physical and emotional—was felt deeply, as we realized our role as protectors had been replaced by his own strength and training. This transformation was both sobering and awe-inspiring, as we witnessed him face adversity head-on, forging a new identity shaped by resilience, sacrifice, and a sense of duty far greater than himself.

**Mom and Dad were miles away, but God was nearby. In our absence, He was present.**

### Terah in College

*Now loving nanny and childcare extraordinaire.*

As the youngest of five sisters, Terah grew up under a specialized form of protection. While her older sisters were each gifted and strong in their own right, they shared one singular, fierce mission: acting as their baby sister's unofficial bodyguards. Her father even wore a T-shirt gifted by the girls that proudly declared, "You can't scare me, I raised five daughters."

That reality shifted the moment Terah moved to a college campus 200 miles away. Suddenly surrounded by a new tribe of friends her family had never met, she finally stepped out from behind the collective shield of her sisters and parents. For the first time, Terah was navigating life's decisions and sidestepping its dangers entirely on her own terms.

The transition to self-reliance was most evident during her trips into the inner-city. For the first time, concerns about her car and her personal safety rested solely on her shoulders. Navigating these urban challenges without the collective shield of her family was a rigorous exercise in situational awareness and a defining part of her journey toward adulthood.

**Mom and Dad were miles away, but God was nearby. In our absence, He was present**

### Teddy's Long Road Home

*Now a father of three and a corporate attorney*

In his youth, Teddy—long before he became Ted J., the attorney —was defined by a winning personality and a natural gift for athletics. His college years took him 1,200 miles from home to the same university where his mother was pursuing her doctorate. As a student-athlete, he played for one of the school's sports teams, a commitment that required him to bridge the massive distance between home and campus four to six times a year.

His car became a mobile sanctuary during those long, solitary stretches of highway. While his father or friends occasionally joined him to share the burden of the drive, the journey's vulnerability was a constant companion. Every mile carried the weight of the "what if"—the looming threat of mechanical failure, accidents, or the unpredictable characters one might encounter at a roadside hotel after dark.

When a sports injury struck, the theoretical independence of college became a practical necessity. For the first time, Ted had to manage his own medical care without a safety net. Far from the familiar support of his parents, he stepped into the role of a self-reliant adult, transforming a physical setback into a crucial leap toward adulthood.

**Mom and Dad were miles away, but God was nearby. In our absence, He was present.**

### How We Survived Those Days

These moments reshaped our understanding of prayer. We realized that God's protection does not depend on our proximity, but on His presence. For years, we had prayed for Him to surround our children with His care, and in the moments when we could do nothing, He did everything. This experience didn't necessarily erase some tragic events or future fears, but it anchored our faith in something far stronger: the reality of God's protection.

### Where is Your Hope Anchored?

The previous chapters introduced a series of questions designed to help you clarify the values you'll carry into this next season of parenting. This final question may be the most vital: Where is your hope anchored?

As a parent, the instinct to protect your child from harm is both natural and necessary. However, every parent eventually reaches a crossroads where protection is no longer possible—where distance, independence, and the complexities of life place decisions beyond your reach. How do you navigate those moments?

Consider the foundations of that hope:

- Hope anchored in achievement eventually leads to disappointment.
- Hope anchored in safety will inevitably be shaken.
- Hope anchored in control will eventually collapse.

In contrast, hope anchored in faith allows you to release specific outcomes while remaining a faithful guide. It facilitates the transition from fear to trust, moving you from a "lifeguard" mentality to that of a "life coach." By loosening your grip, you actually strengthen your influence—shifting from control to a legacy of wisdom, presence, and enduring support.

### Understanding the God Factor

The "God Factor" is the intentional act of weaving faith into the everyday rhythms of parenting. It doesn't require elaborate programs or perfect routines. Instead, it often begins with simple, consistent practices:

- Starting the day with a moment of personal prayer.
- Discussing faith naturally during family meals.
- Reading Scripture together as schedules allow.

These small moments create a vital space for spiritual conversation and reflection. Over time, they reinforce the truth that parenting is not a solo endeavor, but a partnership with the Divine. Just as importantly, these rituals help children recognize that faith is not reserved for a building or a special occasion; it is the heartbeat of daily life.

Through these ordinary habits, children begin to sense a presence in their own lives, seeing firsthand how faith can guide their decisions, their relationships, and their ultimate sense of purpose.

### Psalm 91: A Source of Reassurance

Psalm 91 offers reassurance to parents who seek God as their protector:

> *Whoever goes to the Lord for safety and remains under the protection of the Almighty can say, "You are my defender and protector. You are my God; in You I trust." He will keep you safe from hidden dangers and deadly*

*diseases. He will cover you with His wings, and you will find refuge under His care. His faithfulness will be your shield and defense. You will not fear the dangers of night or the sudden attacks of day... God will command His angels to guard you wherever you go.*

### The Role of Prayer in Parenting

Prayer is the steady pulse of the parenting journey, shaping the atmosphere of the home and the character of the parent. It serves several vital functions:

- **Gratitude:** These prayers help parents pause to celebrate the small joys and everyday blessings inherent in family life.
- **Intercession:** By lifting up a child's safety, needs, and future, parents find peace even when circumstances move beyond their reach.
- **Confession:** This practice allows parents to bring their frustrations and shortcomings before God, trading their anxiety for divine wisdom.

Through these rhythms, we are reminded that parenting is not a solitary task. God remains an active partner in every stage of the journey.

### The Hand-Off: When Faith Becomes Personal

One of the most profound milestones in a family's life often happens without fanfare. It is the "hand-off"—the moment when a child begins to transition from "our faith" to "my faith."

In childhood, faith is often absorbed through the family's ecosystem. Eventually, however, faith must move from a family tradition to a personal conviction. The parents' role in this season is not to force a specific result, but to continue modeling an authentic life of faith while providing the space necessary for the graduate to take ownership of their own beliefs.

### The Journey of Faith and Discovery

As graduates enter adulthood, they face a crossroads that is more internal than external. This season invites them to wrestle with deep questions regarding their identity, purpose, and beliefs. While this stage can feel uncertain for parents, it is a necessary part of spiritual maturity—a time when the values planted years ago begin to guide them in the wider world.

### The Journey of Faith and Discovery

As graduates step into adulthood, they reach a turning point defined more by inner transformation than by new surroundings or routines. Rather than just adjusting to a different city or schedule, they embark on a deeper exploration of who they are and what they believe. This season compels them to examine their identity, purpose, and personal convictions. They sift through the lessons and values of their upbringing, choosing which truly resonate with them. For parents, this stage can feel uncertain, but it is a crucial milestone in spiritual maturity—a time when the values planted years ago begin to guide their journey in the larger world.

### The Value of Questioning

For many young adults, the move toward independence becomes a natural crucible for reflection. As the protective scaffolding of childhood—parents, teachers, and structured communities—recedes, they are left to confront the "why" behind their inherited beliefs. This shift is not just a phase of rebellion; it is a foundational step toward a borrowed identity becoming authentically their own.

. . .

### The Catalyst of Honest Inquiry

Honest questioning is the primary catalyst for this transformation. When a young adult begins to probe the edges of their worldview, they are not necessarily searching for a way out, but for a way in. They are testing the strength of their convictions against the friction of real-world experience.

- **Deconstruction vs. Destruction:** Thoughtful questioning helps remove superficial beliefs that no longer serve a purpose, leaving behind a core that is authentic and personal.
- **Intellectual Ownership:** Beliefs that are never challenged often remain brittle. By engaging difficult questions—about suffering, ethics, or purpose—individuals move from simply "knowing the answers" to truly "understanding the truth.

### Building Resilience for Adult Life

The ultimate goal of this period of reflection is to develop a faith resilient enough to withstand the complexities of adult life. A "vetted" worldview offers a steadier anchor than one accepted solely through tradition.

**Complexity Readiness:** Adult life rarely presents in black-and-white. A resilient faith accounts for nuance and ambiguity, preventing a total collapse of conviction in the face of hardship or contradiction.

**Internal Stability:** Because the individual has already wrestled with their doubts, they are less likely to be blindsided by them later. The "crisis of faith" becomes a "journey of growth."

**Empathetic Engagement:** Those who have questioned their own path are often better equipped to engage with a diverse world. They understand that conviction is a process, not just a destination.

Key takeaway: Doubt is not the enemy of conviction; it is the laboratory where a more durable, authentic self is forged.

### The Power of Witness and Prayer

In moments of complication, the prayers a graduate heard as a child often echo back to them. These memories serve as a reminder that guidance is always available. Eventually, the significance of those spiritual moments begins to "click." They remember when prayer felt real, and God seemed close. This marks the shift from relying on your spiritual life to cultivating their own spiritual life.

As you pray for their journey, ask God to bring other wise counselors into their lives. If you have modeled the value of seeking outside wisdom, they will be better equipped to recognize and welcome the mentors God provides for specific seasons of their growth.

### The Influence of Faithful Community

In a world filled with competing ideologies, a consistent and authentic faith community is a vital anchor. A community that lives out its convictions serves as a "north star" for a graduate navigating unfamiliar waters. When they witness a group of people whose actions align with their message, it reinforces the lessons of their youth. This lived example helps spiritual truths remain rooted as they begin to apply them to their own lives.

As your role shifts from Lifeguard to Life Coach, you naturally become a Spiritual Mentor. In this capacity, you move to the sidelines, offering encouragement and wisdom while your graduate takes the lead in their spiritual journey.

### Expanding Their Horizon

One of the most transformative gifts you can offer a child is the chance to witness faith in action across diverse fields. By introducing them to leaders, artists, and professionals who embody discipline and purpose, you expand their understanding of what a meaningful life can be.

These encounters demonstrate that a career is more than just a climb toward personal ambition; it is a response to a larger calling. As graduates transition into adulthood, they often begin to grapple with a profound shift in perspective:

"The two most important days in your life are the day you are born, and the day you find out why." Attributed to Mark Twain

### From Coach to Greatest Fan

As parents, we have walked our children to the edge of a great horizon. While few eighteen-year-olds can truly chart the course of the marathon ahead, we know that their plans will shift and mature with time. Finding a life's calling is a gradual unfolding, a journey that requires patience but never lacks a destination.

Standing on the sidelines of this new season, our influence takes a different shape. We transition from active coaches to prayerful advocates. Along with asking for their protection, we can seek guidance for their next steps, trusting that they are being steered toward a calling bigger than they can yet see. Your new mission is simple: to be the voice in the stands, cheering them on through it all.

### Your Remaining Heartbeats

As you close this book and watch your graduate move forward, take a moment to pause and consider your own next chapter. While they explore the horizon of who they are becoming, you are stepping into a new season of purpose and influence that is only just beginning.

If you are still guiding younger children toward their own graduations, your mission continues with fresh perspective. However, if this milestone marks the final transition out of your "Lifeguard" years, you now face a profound and personal choice. You stand at a sacred threshold with one vital realization: Your mission as a parent hasn't ended; it has simply evolved.

While you are no longer responsible **for** them, you remain deeply significant **to** them. As you watch them run their race from the stands, remember that you have a race of your own still to run. You have been given the gift of time and the wealth of experience—now, **what will you devote your remaining heartbeats to?**

~

### Parent Reflection Questions:

1. **The Limit of Your Reach:** Can you identify a specific "payphone moment" or "highway mile" in your graduate's life where you felt completely helpless to protect them? How does the realization that God was already there change your current level of anxiety?
2. **Surrendering the Illusion:** In what ways have you been trying to "be God" in your child's life—monitoring, warning, or planning as if you alone are the author of their safety? What would it look like to officially "resign" from that position today?
3. **The Three Pillars:** As you evaluate your graduate's readiness, you've likely looked at their physical health and emotional maturity. How much intentionality have you given to the **Spiritual Pillar**—the sense of meaning that sustains them when the first two pillars are tested?
4. **Hope's Anchor:** Be honest about your foundation: Is your hope currently anchored in your graduate's **achievement**, their **safety**, or your **control**? Which of these is feeling the most "shaken" right now?
5. **The "God Factor" Rhythms:** What is one simple, non-forced habit—like a text of a specific Scripture or a mention of a prayer—that you can weave into your daily

rhythm to signal that faith is the "heartbeat" of your home, not just a Sunday event?

6. **The Spiritual Hand-Off:** How are you handling the transition from "our faith" to "their faith"? Are you providing the necessary space for them to wrestle with deep questions, even if their journey looks different than yours did?
7. **Partnering with the Divine:** If you view yourself as a "Spiritual Co-Parent" with God, what specific burden are you carrying right now that you need to "hand over" to your Partner?
8. **The Power of Witness:** When your graduate looks at your life, do they see a parent whose peace is dependent on their performance, or a parent whose peace is anchored in a "defender and protector"?
9. **Praying for Direction:** Beyond praying for their safety (the Lifeguard's prayer), have you begun praying for their **direction** (the Life Coach's prayer)? Who are the mentors or "wise counselors" you are asking God to bring into their path?
10. **Your Remaining Heartbeats:** As this chapter of daily oversight ends, what is the "Why" for *your* next season? Apart from being a parent, what is the purpose or calling that God is inviting you to devote your remaining energy and heartbeats to?

LOOKING AHEAD: **Help Is Only an Ask Away**

As we reach the conclusion of this journey, we address the final and perhaps most pervasive myth of parenting: the idea that you are meant to navigate the transition to adulthood in total isolation. **Help Is Only an Ask Away** is a call to break the silence of the "Perfect Parent" and embrace the strength found in community. It is a reminder that while the form of your parenting is changing, the need for a "village" remains as vital as ever.

In this final section, we will discuss:

- **The Myth of the Linear Path:** Dismantling the cultural expectation that a "successful" graduate moves seamlessly from a diploma to a high-paying career without a single stumble.
- **Highlight Reel vs. Living Room Reality:** How to protect your heart from the isolation of social media and recognize that every family—even the ones with the polished photos—is navigating the "friction" of adulthood.
- **Vulnerability as a Bridge:** Understanding that when you have the courage to say, "This is hard," you aren't confessing failure—you are handing out a "permission slip" for other parents to drop their masks and offer support.
- **The Four Forms of Support:** Identifying the differences between *Informal* coffee chats, *Communal* small groups, and *Professional* coaching, and how to know which one your family needs right now.

# CHAPTER 10

## HELP IS ONLY AN ASK AWAY

A **Personal Reflection**

What defines a great parent? Too often, we measure our success by outcomes—stable, well-adjusted children who make "good" choices. True parenting, however, is less about the final result and more about the quiet, consistent decisions made in the trenches, day after day. There is no trophy waiting for you when a child reaches adulthood; instead, parenting simply changes form. It becomes a lifelong, evolving journey—one that we and others are traveling alongside you.

**You Are Not Alone**

No parent is meant to navigate this transition in isolation. True support often comes from the "cloud of witnesses" around you: trusted friends, mentors, pastors, counselors, and fellow parents who have already weathered this season.

Asking for help is never a sign of weakness; it is a **mark of wisdom.** When you seek guidance, you model humility for your graduate. You demonstrate that growth doesn't stop at twenty-one and that learning is a lifelong pursuit. Often, the most valuable insights come from those who have already made the mistakes you are currently hoping to avoid.

**Forms of Support**

Help is not one-size-fits-all. It takes many shapes:

- **The Informal:** A heartfelt conversation over coffee or a walk with a friend.
- **The Communal:** Small-group discussions where you realize your "unique" struggle is actually a common experience.
- **The Professional:** Counseling or coaching to navigate complex family dynamics.

The transition from **Lifeguard to Life Coach** is a difficult shift to make in a vacuum. Community offers the perspective, encouragement, and hope necessary when the road feels uncertain.

### Breaking the Silence of "The Perfect Parent"

In our current culture, there is a pervasive and exhausting myth that successful parenting results in a linear, problem-free ascent into adulthood. We are often led to believe that if we did our jobs correctly, our graduates should transition seamlessly from high school to a high-paying career or a prestigious university without a single stumble. This expectation creates a heavy burden of silence, making parents feel that any request for help is actually a confession of failure.

### Social Media Highlight Reel vs. The Living Room Reality

The greatest fuel for this "Perfect Parent" myth is the Social Media Highlight Reel. As you scroll through your feed, you see curated images of dorm room move-ins, graduation parties, and first-job celebrations. What you *don't* see are the late-night arguments about curfews, the anxiety over a stagnant job search, or the quiet "generalized worry" that keeps parents awake at 2:00 AM.

When your daily reality involves a graduate who is "failing to launch" or struggling with the "friction" of adulthood, and your screen is filled with the polished successes of others, a dangerous isolation sets in. You begin to believe that you are the only one struggling. This isolation is where the "Lifeguard" mindset thrives, tempting you to hide the struggle and "rescue" your child in secret rather than coaching them in the light of community.

### VULNERABILITY: The Bridge to Community

To move from isolation to strength, we must realize that Vulnerability is the Bridge to Community. Vulnerability is not about oversharing every family secret; it is about the courage to be seen in your current season.

- **The Permission Slip:** When one parent has the courage to say, *"We are really hitting a wall with our graduate's motivation,"* or *"I'm finding it incredibly hard to let go of the manager role,"* they aren't just seeking help—they are handing out a permission slip. They are giving every other parent in the room the freedom to drop their own mask.
- **From Walls to Bridges:** When we pretend to have it all together, we build a wall that no one can climb. When we admit we are learning, we build a bridge that others can cross.
- **A Shift in Power:** Requesting support signals that your family's health matters more than your public reputation. It turns a solitary struggle into a collaboration.

By breaking the silence, you discover that the "village" you need has been there all along, likely waiting for someone to be brave enough to start the conversation. As a Life Coach, you aren't just preparing your graduate for the world; you are preparing yourself to lead with honesty, showing your child that the strongest people are those who know when to reach for a teammate.

. . .

### Help Is Not a Flaw

Requesting support is not an admission of failure; it is a signal that something matters enough to you to reach beyond your own limitations. When we ask for help, we turn a solitary problem into a **collaboration.** We reduce isolation and accelerate growth. Embracing this vulnerability is an act of courage that creates space for others to give and be seen—an act of care for yourself and the relationships that sustain you.

### We Are Here to Help

If you find yourself wishing someone would walk this season with you, know that you are not alone. The insights in this book come from those who have lived through graduations, detours, successes, and struggles. We have made our share of mistakes, and through them, we have learned that parenting young adults remains one of life's most meaningful callings.

Sometimes, a parent needs more than a chapter; they need a **conversation.** Whether through individual encouragement, prayer, or speaking engagements for your school, church, or community, we are ready to offer practical wisdom. You can find our contact information in the appendix.

There is no shame in seeking guidance, and there is no failure in wanting support. Strong families grow when parents are willing to learn, listen, and lean on others.

~

### Parent Reflectdion Questions:

1. **Redefining the "Trophy":** If parenting success is found in "quiet, consistent decisions" rather than a final outcome, what is one decision you made this week that reflects the character of a great parent, regardless of how your graduate responded?

2. **The Lifelong Journey:** How does the idea that parenting simply "changes form" rather than ending alleviate or increase the pressure you feel right now?
3. **Identifying Your "Cloud":** Who are the "witnesses" in your life—friends, mentors, or counselors—who have already weathered the season you are currently in? When was the last time you reached out to them for perspective?
4. **Modeling Humility:** The text suggests that asking for help models wisdom for your graduate. In what specific area could you show your graduate that you are still "learning and growing" by seeking guidance yourself?
5. **The Myth of the Linear Path:** Have you felt the "heavy burden of silence" caused by the expectation that a graduate's transition should be problem-free? How has this myth affected your willingness to be honest with others?
6. **Highlight Reel vs. Living Room:** Can you identify a moment this week where you felt isolated by social media "successes"? How does acknowledging your "Living Room Reality" help you move toward a Life Coach mindset?
7. **Handing Out the Permission Slip:** Who is one person you trust to whom you can say, "I'm hitting a wall"? How might being vulnerable with them give them the "freedom to drop their own mask"?
8. **Walls vs. Bridges:** Think of your recent interactions with other parents. Were you building a **wall** (pretending to have it all together) or a **bridge** (admitting you are navigating a difficult shift)?
9. **Reputation vs. Health:** The chapter mentions that requesting support signals that your family's health matters more than your public reputation. Is there a specific "struggle" you have been hiding in secret to protect your reputation?
10. **The Collaboration Shift:** How would your stress level change if you viewed your graduate's current "friction" as a

collaboration with a community rather than a solitary failure on your part?

# CONTACT INFO AND RESOURCES

**A Final Note from the Seagos**

Thank you for reading *Parenting the Graduate.* If this book has been a helpful resource for your family, we would love to hear from you.

We are available to speak with parents of graduates in schools, churches, and community settings. Our mission is to encourage families, provide practical tools, and help you navigate the transition from high school to adulthood with confidence and hope.

We invite you to engage with our additional resources to enhance your experience. These are designed to reinforce a vital truth: **you are not alone** as you navigate this transformative season together.

We look forward to connecting with you and supporting you as you guide your graduate into the next chapter of life.

**Connect with us and explore more resources at:** JohnnieandTedSeago.com

**Contact Info:**


- Website: JohnnieandTedSeago.com
- Email: JohnnieandTed@gmail.com

- Social Media: JohnnieandTedSeago

**Resources**

The Seagos offer a variety of resources to support you on your parenting journey. Contact information is found on the johnnieandtedseago.com website.

- **PTG Newsletter:** Receive monthly articles and guidance in a newsletter format.
- **Speaking Engagements:** Opportunities for the Seagos to share insights and experiences with parents of graduates in a school setting, community forum or church.
- **Seminars and Workshops:** Interactive sessions designed to equip parents with practical tools and strategies for navigating the transition from high school to adulthood.
- **Personal Consultations:** One-on-one conversations by phone or in person by appointment to discuss specific concerns and receive tailored advice.
- **Community Connections:** Information on local support groups and networks where you can find encouragement and share experiences with other parents.
- **Online Resources:** Access to articles, videos, and helpful materials on the PTG website to aid in your parenting journey.
- **Social Media Engagement:** Follow the Seagos for ongoing inspiration, tips, and community support through various social media platforms.

**Forms presented in Parenting the Graduate:**

Many of the forms mentioned in Parenting the Graduate can be downloaded and printed. Visit www.johnnieandtedseago.com

# ABOUT THE AUTHORS

**Building a Lasting Legacy**

THROUGH BOOKS, seminars, and coaching, **Drs. Johnnie and Ted Seago** remain focused on one goal: strengthening the pillars of the home. *Parenting the Graduate* is the culmination of their life's work—a roadmap designed to help you celebrate your student's achievement while building a relationship that will thrive for a lifetime.

> "Graduation is not the end of your influence; it is the beginning of a new, profound partnership with your adult child."

With over **four decades of combined experience** in education, leadership, and family ministry, the Seagos offer a unique blend of academic rigor and "in-the-trenches" wisdom. Both hold doctoral degrees in education and have successfully raised eight children—now adults—while delighting in the company of 22 grandchildren.

As career educators who have mentored thousands of families, their expertise encompasses:

. . .

- **Academic & Faith Formation**
  - **Family Life Dynamics**
  - **Practical Life-Skills Coaching**
  - **Parenting Adult Children**

**A Practical, Story-Driven Approach**

The Seagos translate complex research into straightforward tools that parents can implement immediately. Known for their candid storytelling and gentle humor, they leave audiences with **specific next steps** rather than abstract inspiration. They lead workshops and retreats on pivotal topics such as:

- **"Moving from Lifeguard to Life Coach"**
- **Negotiating household agreements for emerging adults**
- **Faithful parenting through major transitions**

**Coaching & Mentorship**

As authors and consultants, the Seagos provide tailored coaching for couples navigating the post-high school transition and mentor young adults entering their next chapter. They also equip local leaders and facilitators to lead parent conversations that reduce conflict and enhance connection.

**Life in Willis, Texas**

Family, church, and community are central to their lives. When not teaching or speaking, Johnnie and Ted enjoy road trips, cheering on their grandchildren, and encouraging young moms and dads to seek a life built on faith and connection.

**Connect with Johnnie and Ted at:** JohnnieandTedSeago.com

www.ingramcontent.com/pod-product-compliance
Lightning Source LLC
LaVergne TN
LVHW090614110826
845146LV00001B/381
* 9 7 9 8 8 9 9 6 2 0 6 8 3 *